WHAT ARE THEY SAYING ABOUT JESUS?

(revised)

What Are They Saying About Jesus?
(revised)

Gerald O'Collins, S.J.

PAULIST PRESS
New York/Ramsey

ACKNOWLEDGMENTS

Chapters 1, 2, 3 and 6 of this book were published in *The Way,* a quarterly review of contemporary Christian spirituality, published by the English Jesuits, under the titles: *Jesus in Current Theology I* and *II* appearing in the issues of October 1976 (Vol. 16, No. 4) and January 1977 (Vol. 17, No. 1). They are reprinted by permission. In somewhat different form the Appendix appeared in *New Blackfriars* (April 1976), *America* (December 20, 1975), and *The Tablet* (December 20, 1975).

Library of Congress
Catalog Card Number: 77-70640

ISBN: 0-8091-2521-8

Published by Paulist Press
545 Island Road, Ramsey, N.J. 07446

Printed and bound in the
United States of America

Contents

Preface

The Second Vatican Council (1962–65) gave its attention to ecclesiastical issues. It produced sixteen documents: on the Church, ecumenism, the liturgy, relations with other religions, the roles of bishops, priests, religious and laity, missionary activity, and the rest. But only secondarily did it consider Christology or doctrines about Jesus Christ.

The experience of the years since the closing of the Council has retaught an old lesson. Any efforts to renew the Church will remain spiritually empty, emotionally hollow and doctrinally unsound unless they draw inspiration and strength from the founder of Christianity himself.

In the original Preface to this book, I suggested: "If Vatican III were to meet in late 1977, its major document would not be 'The Church in the Modern World' but some response to the question: Who is Jesus Christ for us today?" No new Church council has been assembled, but my prediction found its fulfillment in Pope John Paul II's first encyclical, *Redemptor Hominis* (Redeemer of Man),[1] of March 1979. Up to that point in the twentieth century only one papal encyclical was longer (*Mediator Dei* of Pius XII in 1947). None of the earlier encyclicals in our century had taken up the theme of Jesus Christ our Redeemer. They were directed to other topics like the Bible, birth control, celibacy, Christian education, Christian marriage, Christian social doctrines, the Church itself, communism, modernism, the Mother of Jesus, priesthood, and world peace. There was an encyclical establishing the Feast of Christ the King (1925), and another encyclical on devotion to the Sacred Heart (1956). But no Pope had published an encyclical precisely on Christ our Savior, let alone chosen that theme for the first, programmatic statement of his pontificate.

What is the present Pope saying about Jesus? An adequate answer to that question would examine not only *Redemptor Hominis* itself, but also his second encyclical, *Dives in Misericordia* (Rich in Mercy) of 1980, the apostolic exhortation on catechetics of 1979 (*Catechesi Tradendae*), and many of his speeches, especially those dealing with Christ as the ultimate justification for recognizing the inalienable dignity and rights of every human being. Let me note only one point, which will be discussed more fully later. In *Redemptor Hominis* and elsewhere John Paul II refuses to separate the person of Jesus Christ from his saving work. In other words, he takes *who* Christ was/is in himself (= Christology) together with *what* Christ did/does for us (= soteriology).

The witnesses to the new concern for Christology include the Latin American bishops at Puebla in January/February 1979 and the International Theological Commission in 1980. The heart of the final document from Puebla concerns "The Truth about Jesus Christ, the Savior We Proclaim" (nn. 170–219), "The Good News of Jesus Christ and the Church" (nn. 221–231), and "Discerning the Nature of Liberation in Christ" (nn. 480–490). Among many other things, the Puebla document holds together wonderfully well the dying and rising of Christ.

The Christological statements of the International Theological Commission (which will be treated in Chapter 5) have recognized and responded to what was taking place in theology and exegesis. During recent years both academic and popular studies have moved beyond a classic Christology which had maintained its essential structures for well over a thousand years. One thinks here of works by Juan Alfaro, Leonardo Boff, Raymond Brown, James Dunn, Joseph Fitzmyer, Martin Hengel, Walter Kasper, Hans Küng, René Latourelle, James Mackey, Jürgen Moltmann, Malcolm Muggeridge, Wolfhart Pannenberg, Karl Rahner, John Robinson, Rosemary Ruether, Edward Schillebeeckx, Piet Schoonenberg, Jon Sobrino, Sally TeSelle, and the whole group who have continued to contribute to the "new quest" for the historical Jesus. I am putting aside scruples here and pulling in names almost at random. But these and other authors serve to illustrate the shift since the early 1960's. In one way or another they all seek to provide fresh help toward answering the questions: Where can we find Jesus Christ today? How should we interpret him for ourselves and for others?

Over the last decades more and more Church leaders, theologians and other Christians have come to acknowledge and grapple with a basic truth. At any critical moment in world history—and every moment in history brings its special crisis—questions of ecclesiastical theory and practice will never be satisfactorily resolved unless we go back to our understanding of Jesus himself. What we *do* with the Church will be ultimately conditioned by what we think about Jesus, and vice versa. There is always a mutual relationship between ecclesiology (the theory and practice of the Church) and Christology. The Church in the world is the place where Christians worship, act and suffer. It is Jesus Christ who gives point and purpose to what they do and endure.

I have set myself several tasks in this book. First of all, I plan to indicate six themes in classical Christology that no longer satisfy and have prompted the search for new approaches. This classical Christology essentially followed the Council of Chalcedon (A.D. 451), which provided the Church with its traditional accounts of Jesus Christ as one person in two natures. Then Chapters 2 and 3 will discuss some key characteristics of recent views. Chapter 4 takes up in detail the Christologies of three contemporary authors: Mackey, Sobrino and Schillebeeckx. Chapter 5 looks at statements on Christology from the International Commission. The final chapter argues that popular writers may express more vividly something obscured at times by the scholars—the religious appeal of Jesus. After an epilogue the book ends with an appendix which contains an exploratory study on the imagination of Jesus.

The complete revision and updating of this book was begun in West Germany and completed in Italy. I wish to dedicate it affectionately to some Roman friends (Enrico, Giorgio, Jack, Liliana, Maria Franca, Mimi and Pino), and to those wonderful hosts and ministers of the Lord, the German Jesuits of Caritas Pirckheimer

House in Nuremberg. For various kinds of help in producing this work my warm thanks go out to Paul Conroy, Michael Culhane, Kathy Halvey and Don Sharp.

The Gregorian University, Rome   *Gerald O'Collins, S.J.*
August 19, 1982

1
Classical Christology Under Fire

Six headings gather together the major reasons for a recent swing away from the classical Christology developed by many earlier generations of theologians. It is (1) a Christology 'from above', which (2) remains incarnation-centered, (3) runs into philosophical problems, (4) mixes together historical, theological and mythical language, (5) bypasses the ministry of Jesus, and (6) separates the person of Jesus Christ from his work, that is to say, separates Christology from soteriology or the doctrine of salvation.

At once some readers may already feel uneasy with this list of reasons. What is wrong, for instance, with a Christology that 'remains incarnation-centered'? Surely the feasts of the annunciation and Christmas encourage us to see the high point of all human history as God becoming man? Yet let us at least give the reasons a hearing. Only then can we respond to them with sympathy and understanding, even if we do not leap headlong to embrace them.

(1) 'He descended from heaven' serves as the starting point for the Christology of Thomas Aquinas, Karl Barth and other classic theologians. This Christology 'from above' bothers many of our contemporaries. They are troubled not so much by any mythological picture of 'a coming down' from some heavenly realm. The more fundamental trouble is that this classic Christology *begins from God*. Its opening question assumes the form: How does God become man? How does the pre-existent Son of God enter our world?

This way of formulating the initial approach brings with it two difficulties. First, it has often seemed to cast doubt on the genuinely human existence of Jesus. The figure in the manger may cry like any baby. He may grow up seemingly just another boy playing on the streets of Nazareth. He may preach in the style of a wandering rabbi. The Roman forces of occupation can put him to death by that hideous combination of impalement and display which they called crucifixion. But all the same we know he is really God and this injects an element of make-believe into the whole life-story from Bethlehem on. He looks like a man, speaks like a man, suffers and dies like a man. But underneath he is divine, and this makes his genuine humanity suspect. Is he no more than God in disguise? This first difficulty with the classical Christology 'from above' runs along lines suggested by Christmas pantomimes. Daisy looks something like a cow and moos better than most cows. But all through the act we know she is no real cow at all. Right from the manger does Jesus simply play at the role of being a man?

The other difficulty about the opening question ('*How* does God become man?') arises from the answer given by the Greek Fathers of the Church to the related question 'Why?': God becomes man in order that man might become God. The possibility of imitating and sharing the divine nature seemed easier to grasp during the early centuries of the Christian era. Today it is not simply the silence or 'felt' absence of God which makes the old theme less plausible. Man knows himself to be dehumanised in so many ways. He needs first to feel humanised before he can dream of being divinised. Man has to be 'incarnated' before he can bear to talk about the incarnation of a divine person.

(2) This brings us to the major 'mystery' in the Christology 'from above'. This kind of Christology takes *the incarnation* to be the central doctrine about Jesus Christ. Its reflections start from the nativity, not from the events of Good Friday and Easter Sunday. What happens after the incarnation becomes little more than the mere unfolding of all that has already taken place at the incarnation itself. Chalcedon encouraged this approach. The key statement from that council centered on the incarnation, and mentioned neither the crucifixion nor the resurrection.

Along with Pannenberg and other recent writers, Kasper sets his face against such an

> incarnation-oriented Christology. If we allow that the divine-human person of Jesus is constituted once and for all through the incarnation, then the history and fate of Jesus—above all his cross and resurrection—have no more constitutive meaning. The death of Jesus is then merely the completion of the incarnation. The resurrection is no more than the confirmation of the divine nature.[2]

It is not that the doctrine of the incarnation should be given up. But the New Testament suggests that thinking about Jesus Christ should begin elsewhere.

St. Paul occasionally speaks of the Son's pre-existence (Gal 4, 4; Rom 8, 3), but he takes the incarnation as no more than the prerequisite to the central mystery. The nativity as such neither saves us nor can it serve as the baseline for our further reflection. Paul's starting point is always Christ's saving death and resurrection. He implies that we should think of Christmas in the light of Easter, not vice versa. He offers us an elaborate list of resurrection witnesses (1 Cor 15, 5-8). But he passes over Christ's nativity in almost total silence. We hear from him no more than that Christ was born into a Jewish family (Gal 4, 4) who belonged to the house of King David (Rom 1, 3).

Paul's thinking about the sacraments ties in with his basic approach to Christ. Baptism draws believers into the crucifixion and gives them promise of resurrection (Rom 6, 3-5). We are not baptised 'into the incarnation'. The Eucharist proclaims the death of the risen Lord until he comes in glory (1 Cor 11, 26). We do not celebrate the Eucharist to proclaim the birth of Christ until he grows to manhood.

Paul's letters written from the late 40s to the early 60s made him our earliest New Testament author. When he composed his gospel around 65, St. Mark began with the baptism of Christ and left us a work which has been often described as a passion story with a long introduction. Good Friday and Easter Sunday brood over this gospel which included no nativity or incarnation stories. When they wrote later with Mark's gospel in front of them, Matthew and Luke decided to start with stories of Jesus' birth and childhood. Finally, St. John towards the close of the first century began his gospel with the sublime proclamation: 'The Word became flesh and dwelt amongst us, and we saw his glory, the glory of the only-begotten Son of the Father' (1, 14). The movement from Paul through the first three gospels to John represented an increasing concern to clarify Jesus' origins. This movement continued beyond the age of the apostles. The early centuries of controversy about Christ's identity culminated in Chalcedon's confession that Christ was one person in two natures.

If we wish to make some progress in our own wrestling with the mystery of Christ, we need to follow for ourselves the direction in which Christian thinking originally went. We must begin with the Easter Jesus, not with the Christmas Jesus. The classical Christology involves an unworkable, as well as an unbiblical, plan of attack. It reflects on what Christ was from the beginning rather than on what he did at the end. This condemns it to tortured and frustrating attempts to relate Christ's humanity and divinity within one personal existence. That brings us to the third major problem with the classical approach.

(3) By starting from the Chalcedonian confession, classical Christology instantly commits itself to endless wrestling with the questions: What terms—be they strictly or only loosely *philosophical*—should we use to relate in a true unity the being human and the being divine in Christ? How can we state the double reality of 'true God and true man', so that one aspect does not prevail at the expense of the other? This way into Christology sows dragons' teeth which instantly spring up as fully-armed problems to block our way forward.

First, *either* (a) the being human and the being divine co-exist in a dubious unity, *or* else (b) a credible humanity gets edged out for the sake of insisting on Christ's divinity. The first alternative fails to match the very council to which appeal is made. Chalcedon's confession dwells insistently on the oneness of Christ's person. In an almost literal sense, its first and last words about Jesus Christ are that he is one.

Alternative (b) has been adopted in practice by most theologians, tolerated by Church leaders and believed by vast numbers of the faithful. As Erik Routley remarks, 'traditionally an over-emphasis on the humanity has always tended to lead to positions that the church labelled as eccentric; an over-emphasis on the divinity has led to positions which were comfortably accommodated within orthodoxy.'[3] Nevertheless, such an imbalance plays false to Chalcedon itself and the pope who loomed over the council. Leo the Great insisted: 'It is as dangerous an evil to deny the truth of the human nature in Christ as to refuse to believe that his glory is equal to that of the Father' (Sermon 27, 1).

Second, Chalcedon introduced terminology from (popular) Greek philosophy in speaking of 'one person in two natures'. Of course, it neither intended to replace the New Testament message by such terminology, nor set out to define exactly what the divine nature and the human nature are. Nevertheless, the two terms (nature and person) can leave us smothered with difficulties.

Take the *two-natures* teaching. Only too easily it can suggest a Christ divided into a divine and a human layer—a double being with two natures juxtaposed. 'One person in two natures' sounds almost like a man in two jobs or someone with dual nationality. The terminology obscures the dramatic difference between being human and being divine. The 'job' of being divine is radically other than the 'job' of being human. Divine 'nationality' is worlds away from human 'nationality'.

It costs little time to ferret out the difficulties that cluster around 'person'. Even though Chalcedon did *not* call Christ a 'divine person', traditional theology has interpreted its confession in that sense. Christ is not a human person, but a divine person who assumed human nature without assuming human personality. But, as Schoonenberg argues, can Christ be completely human if he is not a human person? To deny his human personhood seems tantamount to denying that he is man. Moreover, nothing can be done to conceal the real shift between the ancient and modern concepts of 'person'. Classical theology spoke of a rational being existing in its own right. It failed to express interpersonal relations in its account, 'an individual substance of a rational nature (*naturae rationalis individua substantia*)'. Modern thought latches onto self-awareness, freedom and—in a particular way—intersubjectivity as key characteristics of a personhood. We become persons in dealing with other persons, sharing a common language and experiencing a common history. Human persons exist only in the plural. We repeat the traditional word ('person') at our peril. It has changed its meaning.[4]

(4) The fourth way in which traditional Christology has looked inadequate concerns its easy acceptance of that mixture of history, faith and mythical imagery which the old creeds present. The statements run, one after the other, as follows:

> Christ was conceived by the Holy Ghost,
> born of the Virgin Mary,
> suffered under Pontius Pilate,
> was crucified, died and was buried;
> he descended into hell;
> he rose again from the dead;
> he ascended into heaven.

The simple listing together of these items can conceal the fact that we are constantly shifting from one order to another. Where does 'ordinary' history begin and end? It is no surrender to nervous trendiness to point out that the crucifixion belongs to the order of public history, whereas an ascension into heaven does not. To accept that Jesus was born of Mary and suffered under Pontius Pilate does not demand Christian faith. But ony a believer will admit that Jesus was conceived by the Holy Ghost.

Küng reminds his readers that Christ's resurrection may not be presumed to be of the same order as the virginal conception, the descent into hell and the ascension, simply because the Apostles' Creed takes all these articles of faith together. He points out that 'the oldest New Testament witness, the apostle Paul, says nothing about virgin birth, descent into hell and ascension. But with inexorable decisiveness he takes the resurrection of the Crucified One as the centre of Christian preaching.'[5]

(5) The fifth objection deals with a startling omission in much traditional Christology. Like the Apostles' Creed that Christology jumps straight from 'born of the Virgin Mary' to 'suffered under Pontius Pilate'. It undermines its usefulness by simply bypassing the history of Jesus' ministry.

Thomas Aquinas and other medieval theologians attended to

the 'mysteries' of Christ's life. But in recent centuries Christology became impoverished by losing its capacity to think about the great features of the ministry. Even such a recent and innovative work as Pannenberg's *Jesus—God and Man* (1964) disconcertingly ignored the miracles and other prominent themes of Jesus' life. Pannenberg dwelt on the claims to authority, but showed no interest in providing some 'personality profile' of Jesus. Moltmann's *Theology of Hope* (1964) passed over the ministry in almost total silence. Despite that book's sharp polemic against Rudolf Bultmann, it did not effectively part ways with his reduction to a minimum of the theological importance of Jesus' history. As a classical spokesman for such an approach, Kierkegaard long ago expressed the conviction that Christology need find nothing very urgent or interesting to say about the historical existence of Jesus: 'If the contemporary generation [of Jesus] had left nothing behind them but these words: "We have believed that in such and such a year God appeared among us in the humble figure of a servant, that he lived and taught in our community, and finally died," it would be more than enough.'[6]

Kasper, Küng, Schillebeeckx, Moltmann in his *The Crucified God* (1972) and other recent authors include lengthy sections on the history of Jesus. What we witness here is not a determination on the part of theologians to appear absolutely up with the latest results coming in from their colleagues engaged in purely biblical studies. Rather they refuse to take their cue from the ancient creeds of the Church and leap straight from the incarnation to the passion. What should have been obvious has come as a grand discovery. The ministry must claim attention in any serious study of Jesus Christ.

(6) Finally, much theology that took its inspiration from Chalcedon managed to separate Christology from soteriology, and felt happy to consider the person of Christ apart from his saving 'work'.

To be sure, the ancient creeds of the Church confessed the cause of Christ's 'descent from heaven' to be 'for us men and for our salvation'. Moreover, the historical setting of Chalcedon makes it clear that a deep concern for redemption lay behind the discussions of Christ's divine and human nature. The long struggle to defend and clarify his status as 'true God and true man' aimed at preserving the reality of salvation. Any tampering with either component was understood to undermine the experienced truth of redemption. If Jesus were not truly God, he would not have liberated us to share in the divine life. If he were not truly man, he would not have taken hold of and saved human life in all its fullness.

Nevertheless, the Chalcedonian teaching on the two natures seemingly 'represents Christ to us merely as an object of knowledge'. 'Such a view', Schoonenberg continues, 'detaches Christology from soteriology. This objection holds for many christological treatises which, as formal elaborations of the *unio hypostatica,* are completely distinct from soteriology.'[7] Too often Christology simply lapsed into a mass of abstract and cliché-burdened teachings about the divine-human constitution of Christ. It simply slipped out of view that not just 'Saviour' but all the other titles used of Jesus in the New Testament express aspirations for salvation. It was likewise forgotten that behind the Christological statements of the early Church we find soteriological themes. Today, however, few would disagree with Kasper's insistence that we need to overcome this separation between the person and work, between what Jesus is in himself (*in se*) and what he is for us (*pro nobis*), between the so-called ontological and a functional approach. *How* Kasper's ideal is to be realized is another question, to which we return in the third chapter.

2
New Christological Themes

Thus far we have glanced quickly at certain features of traditional Christology which no longer win acquiescence from modern theologians. Inevitably such a rapid survey does less than justice to some aspects of the past. It is only too easy to caricature our theological forefathers and win merely pyrrhic victories over straw men. Granted, however, that some of the criticisms stick, what does the best current writing about Jesus Christ offer as a replacement? Here, as elsewhere, there is little point in exchanging one inadequate situation for another. Let us then examine what fresh lines of attack have emerged in contemporary Christology.

(1) Almost all contemporary thinking about Jesus Christ begins not 'from above' but 'from below'. It takes as its starting point (a) man, (b) the created cosmos, (c) history, or (d) some combination of all three elements. Its initial questions assume the form: What does it mean to say that a particular man was and is both universal Saviour and God-among-us? How could a man be such and be recognizable as such?

Where this Christology 'from below' chooses (a) for its way in, it may follow Küng's lead and study the experience, ideologies and faiths of human beings in the late twentieth century before going on to consider what the gospels indicate about the earthly existence of Jesus.[8] Or a Christology 'from below' may simply go straight to the humanity of Jesus. In both cases some anthropology or doctrine of man will shape the discussion. Catholic theologians may support their approach by pointing to *Gaudium et Spes* and other documents

13

which made Vatican II the first Church council ever to deal explicitly with anthropological issues before going on to strictly theological matters. Protestant theologians may complement or introduce their Christological reflections with studies entitled *Man* (Moltmann) or *What Is Man?* (Pannenberg). It requires no special enlightenment to read off a common concern on both sides of the denominational divide. Scholars share the conviction that we can find and fashion ways of understanding Jesus, only if we attentively re-evaluate the nature of humanity itself. Christology is not proving oddly different here. An orientation towards man characterizes all the branches of contemporary theology.

Nowadays the idea that man is a changing and developing being surfaces right across the whole spectrum of human studies and theories. The process philosophy of Alfred North Whitehead, various Marxist ideologies, evolutionary humanism and all kinds of theses that stress the dynamic element in man agree at least in this. Man is a being on the way rather than a finished product, a future-oriented being who ceaselessly moves beyond himself rather than a completed essence fixed once and for all. It is against the background of such dynamic views that we now call Jesus 'true man'.

Christology 'from below' takes place in a world of thought that has been led in new directions by Darwin, Marx, Freud, Durkheim, John Stuart Mill and a host of other pioneers. The human sciences have taught us all to appreciate man in his many-faceted sociological, psychological and political dimensions. Theologians can hardly be expected to forget all this schooling once they turn to consider Jesus of Nazareth. It would be schizoid to inhabit one world as a result of one's seminary training and another world as a result of one's university studies.

Duquoc introduces sociological interpretation and psychoanalytic theories in his two-volume work, *Christologie, essai dogmatique.*[9] Whatever our verdict on the merits of this particular Christology 'from below', it exemplifies the need not only to recognise and affirm in Jesus the fullness of human existence, but also to do that in a world of thought shaped by the human sciences. Once we agree that as a genuine human being Jesus developed psychologically, we cannot then ignore Freud, Jung and Erikson by refusing even to raise the question: What could that development have been like—before and after puberty?

Instead of, or as well as, starting from considerations about (a) human existence, a Christology 'from below' may choose to begin from (b) the whole created *cosmos* or (c) from the *history* of the world. (b) Teilhard de Chardin interpreted the appearance of Christ within his scheme of evolutionary optimism. As the whole of creation moved dynamically forward and upward, Christ marked a unique leap from the lower level of matter towards a higher spiritual unity. (c) History plays a large role in the Christologies 'from below' developed by Moltmann and Pannenberg. In taking the crucified Jesus as the origin of all Christian theology, Moltmann develops a Christology situated 'after Auschwitz' and within the whole *history of suffering*.[9a] Pannenberg endorses the Hegelian principle that the truth is in the whole. Universal history becomes the place to look when we seek the truth about Jesus of Nazareth. His resurrection anticipates the end of world history and allows us to find in his destiny the revelation of God. History—whether the history of suffering, universal history or some other version of history—can offer perspectives from which to organize the material taken into one's Christology.

Whichever precise way it runs, a Christology 'from below' will probably safeguard the genuine human existence of Jesus. But will it compel us to push beyond his created humanity and confess, 'My Lord and my God'? What was so special about him when set over against the great prophets, the martyred Socrates or the finest among the ancient rabbis? Classical Christology 'from above' could quickly lay its finger on the distinctive element. The Word of God was incarnate in Jesus the man. Current Christology 'from below', however, may point to the supreme love shown by Jesus, his 'being for others,' his sinlessness, or his being 'the unique, *supreme*, case of the total actualization of human reality'.[10] 'Face' has become a favorite word to express the special factor. Küng speaks of 'God with the face of Jesus'.[11] John Robinson chose *The Human Face of God* as the title for his Christology, and Schillebeeckx sums up his conclusions as follows: 'Jesus of Nazareth reveals in his own person the eschatological face of all humanity, and in so doing discloses the Trinitarian full-

ness of God's unity of being, as in its essence and in absolute freedom
a gift to man.'[12]

Any of these Christologies 'from below' crashes into a perennial
problem here. Do they say enough to justify us calling Jesus 'true
man *and true God*'? Mere sinlessness or being 'the man for others'
fails to take us that far. Likewise, the supreme divine revelation
could take place through the person of Jesus without our needing to
agree that in looking on his face we are literally looking on the face
of God. The agent of divine revelation cannot automatically be assumed to be identical with God.

Debates between Christologies 'from above' and Christologies
'from below' can leave us fretting over charges and counter-charges
about pastoral responsibility, fidelity to Chalcedon and the rest. Several years ago I wrongly participated in such polemics. A conservative theologian hit out at Küng: 'He is driving people out of the
Church by not stating clearly that Christ was and is God.' I struck
back: 'Others have driven people out of the Church by not stating
clearly that Christ was and is man.'

Both Christologies have their difficulties. On balance, however,
most contemporary theologians prefer to attempt a Christology
'from below' and practise Augustine's principle, 'Through the man
Christ you move to the God Christ' (Sermon 261, 7).

(2) Unlike theologians of the past, many practitioners of Christology 'from below' centre on the *death and resurrection*. Not all,
however. Karl Rahner describes the incarnation as the 'climax' in
'the total history of the human race'. In his view, the death and resurrection of Christ, being already 'implied and accepted' at the outset, turn out to be an unfolding of 'the absolute mystery of the
incarnation'.[13] Others like John Robinson in effect make evolving
creation itself the primary focus. He insists that Jesus was, 'with the
rest of us, a genuine product of the evolutionary process'. The star-
dust at the foundation of the world prepared the way for the coming
of Jesus.[14] Here one detects, peeping over Robinson's shoulder, the
looming figure of Teilhard. The bishop's *Human Face of God* includes some remarks on Jesus' resurrection, but bypasses Calvary to
the point that neither 'cross' nor 'crucifixion' appears in the index.
The book makes nothing of the fact that the human face of God became disfigured and silent at Calvary.[14a]

Where Rahner and Robinson focus—respectively—on the incarnation and creation, others like Küng revert to the ministry of Jesus as the heart of the matter. It is not that Küng neglects to discuss the events of Good Friday and Easter Sunday. But he seems most at home with Jesus' activity as preacher and healer. With deep and serious feeling he analyses the Sermon on the Mount, the new commandment of love, the miracles and other gospel themes which offer the clearest possible picture of Jesus as he actually lived and impressed himself on his hearers.

Given that we have no decisive consensus, does it really matter where a Christology 'from below' finds its central focus? Why not latch onto creation, the incarnation, the ministry or even the final coming of Christ? Such a tolerant pluralism will not work, at least not if we wish to share the central New Testament approach. The first Christians knew themselves to be healed and graced as a result of those days when the Lord 'was put to death for our trespasses and raised for our justification' (Rom 4, 25). Through faith and baptism they enjoyed the power which flowed from the paschal mystery. They were not 'baptised into' the creation, the ministry of Jesus or his final coming. Not that they devalued these further aspects of their total belief. But they found in the resurrection of their crucified Lord the centre from which they looked forward and backward to the other mysteries of faith.

(3) Earlier we noted some difficulties that confront classical Christology in its use of language and philosophical terminology. Any Christology from below would only be bluffing if it pretended to avoid all such terminology and its attendant difficulties. Kasper rightly requires that every Christology must be properly philosophical. Any serious discussion of Jesus Christ brings us into the deep water where we confront the final meaning of reality and the most basic needs of man. An undertow of philosophical issues tugs at Christology from start to finish. The ultimate and universal quality of the questions raised by the life, death and resurrection of Jesus demands that we accept help from philosophers. We cannot satisfy this demand by using sociology and other human sciences. If we remove philosophy at one point, we will find it coming back at another.

Schillebeeckx and Schoonenberg exemplify the way philosophical questions inevitably surface in any worthwhile account of Jesus

Christ. A sentence from Schillebeeckx was quoted above: 'Jesus of Nazareth reveals in his own person the eschatological face of all humanity.' Obviously we move straight into philosophical discussion, once we ask for the meaning of 'person', 'revelation' and 'humanity'. And what counts as an 'eschatological face'? Schoonenberg argues for a Christology of 'presence'. Philosophy necessarily intrudes once we start to question the nature of this presence. Are we dealing with the mutual presence of passengers on a rush-hour bus? Or the presence of parents with their children? Or some presence of God experienced by those gathered for worship? As soon as we seek to sort out just what these and other kinds of presence ultimately entail, we move into genuinely philosophical analysis.

In the past, Greek philosophy, both directly or more often in a diluted form, helped theological musings and at times even held them together. Some theologians may have refused to espouse Aristotle's four causes, doctrines about 'prime matter' and reflections on 'substance and accidents'. Nevertheless, to a degree all shared in the one perennial philosophy deriving ultimately from the Greeks. In the last century or so things have fallen apart, even if much debris from that perennial philosophy still lies around.

A new philosophical pluralism affects Christology no less than any other branch of theology. Schillebeeckx mixes Thomism, existentialism and some elements from linguistic philosophy. Boff draws on Marxist and Teilhardian themes. Hegelian terminology pops up frequently in Kasper's *Jesus the Christ* to betray his heritage from German idealism.

What forces itself on our attention here is the constant need for philosophical awareness. At times traditional Christology used debased philosophical language which was hideous and empty of meaning. Contemporary Christology can fail in stringency and coherence. Küng's *On Being a Christian* serves to illustrate this.

Küng rightly draws attention to the rich variety of ways in which piety, literature, theology, art and Church teaching have represented Christ. He asks: 'Which is the true picture of Christ?' He then introduces a give-away comparison: 'Too many different and possibly touched-up photographs of one and the same person can make detective work difficult. And detective work—often one of the most exciting and tense efforts at discovery—is again and again a

really considerable part of Christian theology.'[15] He presses on to offer a long discussion entitled 'The Real Christ'.[16] He warns us to be
ready for surprises as we join him in the task of detection and look
for 'the original Jesus'.[17]

Three things make Küng's method suspect. First, he seems to
presuppose that some *one* picture or description will give us the true
Jesus. This premise ignores the fact that, in describing persons, indef-
initely many true accounts are possible. It would be nonsense to line
up all Rembrandt's self-portraits and after a careful comparison select one as the only true picture of the artist. Are we to scrutinize all
the literature about Napoleon on the supposition that we can finally
hold up just one biography and declare, 'That's the real Napoleon'?
Various portraits, accounts and biographical reflections can all be
describing the same person truly. Some say more and others less. We
will expect a number of common pictures. But we may not compare
and contrast them on the grounds that only one will turn out to be
the genuine 'photograph' of the person in question.

Second, I am not convinced that Küng sufficiently alerts his
readers to the irreducible difference between (a) Jesus Christ *in himself* and (b) *any* picture, idea or description Küng and others may
have *of him*. We can use the gospels, traditional faith and practice,
and our own experience to check and correct our description of Jesus. But we may never reduce 'the real Christ' even to our most carefully formed and cherished picture of him.

Third, analogies should not, of course, be expected to indicate
all that is involved. Nevertheless, the comparison with detective
work risks implying that our study of Jesus and his history can be
pressed into the mould of some neutral science of detection. Not only
in the case of Jesus but in the study of history generally the past becomes present only as something conditioned by one's personal attitudes. My set of beliefs must inevitably colour any interpretation of
Karl Marx, Oliver Cromwell or Abraham Lincoln. Both Küng's
comparison with detective work and other material in his book (to
which we will return later) can imply a spurious objectivity in historical investigation. It is dangerous to suggest that we can act like
detectives—hunting through the available materials and using some
special scientific skills until we finally seize the *real* Jesus, faster and,
so to speak, more objectively than others. Add, too, that perennial

conviction and experience of Christians. *We* do not hunt down Jesus. He is the divine detective tracking us down. We find him because he has first found us.

(4) The fourth complaint we considered in the first chapter came from traditional Christology's failure to sort out history, mythical imagery and theological belief in the various doctrines about Christ listed in the Apostles' Creed. We can sample some of contemporary Christology's contributions here.

Few readers, I suspect, will be troubled by Küng's remarks on the ascension. But many will be upset by what he maintains about the virginal conception of Jesus. First, the ascension. Küng points out that the story about the risen Lord being taken up into the sky before the eyes of his followers (Acts 1, 9-11) has a double function: to mark the end of the 'ordinary' Easter appearances,[18] and to introduce the Church's mission which will last until the Lord comes again. The ascension was not in fact a separate happening in its own right, but an aspect of the total Easter-event. Luke communicates his message by means of a story.[19] Only fundamentalists will insist that forty days after the resurrection the Lord literally 'took off' for heaven from the Mount of Olives and then two angels came to send the disciples home to Jerusalem.

On the virginal conception Küng draws attention to the silence of Mark, Paul and John. They proclaim Jesus as Son of God, without ever mentioning the virginal conception. They believe that the appearance of Jesus meant a startlingly new situation for mankind and the world. But accepting this today, Küng suggests, may not be made easier by 'the legend' of a miraculous conception. 'No one', he argues, 'can be obliged to believe in the biological fact of a virginal conception.'[20]

If many Catholics will find this position helpful and liberating, others will angrily part ways with Küng here: 'Having demythologized papal infallibility, he now turns on the Virgin Mary. Where will it all stop?' Ultimately, however, any discussion can settle down and become fruitful only if we agree to change our fundamental question from '*Where* will it all stop?' to '*How* do we stop?' *How* should we go about interpreting the scriptures and traditional belief on this or that point? What principles should we apply in this task of 'faith seeking understanding'?

Any serious reflection on the virginal conception would mean indulging an enormous parenthesis. Interested readers might consult Raymond Brown's valuable treatment.[21] I must, however, confess some misgivings about Brown's language and presuppositions. At the end of a careful and reasonable look at material from scripture, traditional teaching and theology, Brown sums up: 'My judgment, in conclusion, is that the totality of the *scientifically controllable* evidence leaves an unresolved problem—a conclusion that should not disappoint since I used the word "problem" in my title.'[22] But do the connotations of the word 'problem' somewhat prejudice matters right from the outset? In handling such doctrines as Christ's virginal conception, resurrection, ascension and presence in the Eucharist, we do not engage in problem-solving but enter the area of mystery. To be sure, a rational investigation of Church tradition and good exegesis of the New Testament texts are necessary, but they are not sufficient. Will 'scientifically controllable' evidence alone ever prove decisive as regards, let us say, Christ's presence in the Eucharist? What would count as evidence here? What kind of science stands behind the words 'scientifically controllable'? Perhaps I am being unduly fussy. Yet, granted that it would be wrong to take Christ's resurrection as 'a problem' to be discussed on the basis of 'the totality of the scientifically controllable evidence', what allows us to approach the virginal conception in that way?[23]

(5) Recently theologians have remedied their predecessors' neglect by introducing material from *Jesus' ministry* as essential for any adequate Christology. But, to put it mildly, the ministry of Jesus is no simple, easily grasped phenomenon. Three themes can be singled out for particular attention: (a) the Christology implicit in the ministry, (b) Jesus as the 'principle' for criticising the Church, and (c) his language as a key to his imagination.

(a) For fifty years or more debates have raged about Jesus' sense of his personal identity. Did he know himself to be *and* call himself Messiah, Son of God, Son of Man and Suffering Servant? If so, what meaning did he attach to those notions in evaluating and revealing himself? At times these debates moved from the historical record, as far as it is recoverable, to the area of principle. *Could* Jesus have *been* Son of God and Messiah without knowing that clearly or at least without in some way being aware of that? Is such a separation between the order of *being* (his actual identity) and the order of *knowl-edge* (his self-awareness) tolerable and plausible?

Bruce Vawter, for instance, blends history and principle to make his point in this debate:

> To say that Jesus in his earthly life knew and judged him-self to be God's natural Son and very God is to assert the *unprovable* and, from the perspective of the New Testa-ment, the improbable. Had Jesus known such a thing he *could hardly* have contained his knowledge, yet the gospels are witness that his most intimate disciples did not recog-nize his essential relation to God prior to the resurrection.[24]

We can unpack the argument. Even if X (Jesus' knowing and judging 'himself to be God's natural Son and very God') were the case, we could never prove it. Besides if X were the case, then Y: Jesus 'could hardly' have kept this to himself. But we have no evidence that he ever blurted out this secret. Therefore, X was not the case. The real issue here, of course, touches Vawter's theological and/or philosoph-ical grounds for claiming that X is 'unprovable', and that, if X, then Y 'could hardly' have failed to take place. Such argumentation has obviously shifted out of the field of 'mere' exegesis.

Many exegetes, however, have been content to subject certain texts to repeated and minute scrutiny. Did Jesus really say 'The Son of Man also came not to be served but to serve, and to give his life as a ransom for many' (Mk 10, 45)? If these were in fact his words, was he consciously identifying himself as both the Son of Man (Dan 7, 13f.) and the Suffering Servant of Isaiah? Did he mean to distinguish himself from the Son of Man in glory? Or take that 'Johannine mete-orite fallen on the Synoptic earth', a saying that at first glance sug-gests the 'high' doctrine of divine Sonship one finds in the fourth gospel: 'No one knows the Son except the Father, and no one knows the Father except the Son and anyone to whom the Son chooses to reveal him' (Mt 11, 27). Does this verse not only come from Jesus himself, but also imply an uniquely exclusive way of being God's Son?

Such discussions moved in one way or another around the topic of Christological *titles*, their meaning and their use or non-use by Jesus and his contemporaries. Some scholars like Geza Vermes in *Jesus the Jew* continue to keep the issue of titles alive. This study leads to the conclusion that Jesus' intimates and even his less committed admirers venerated him as Prophet, Lord and Son of God.

Recently, however, more stress has been laid on the *general attitudes* of Jesus as a key to the way he identified himself. Thus Küng refuses to begin by examining the titles which might 'go back' to the ministry of Jesus. We will only get into a mess if our arguments for Jesus' self-understanding rest on a debatable conclusion about some one title or particular verse. Apologists have made much, for instance, of the interchange between Jesus and the high priest during the trial. Yet they had to establish that Jesus replied to the question 'Are you the Christ, the Son of God' (Mt 26, 64) with a straight 'I am' (Mk 14, 62). His answer did not take a non-committal form, 'The words are yours' (Mt 26, 64). Moreover, apologists needed to prove that somehow the disciples had access to the trial proceedings and faithfully reported the master's self-description on that occasion. Rather than get trapped in such debates, Küng points rather to the broad and undeniable characteristics of the ministry.[25]

The preaching of Jesus implied a stunning claim to authority. At times he called the Mosaic law into question, put himself above that law and spoke in God's place. A willingness to lose his life and act as the servant of all drove him to associate with tax agents, prostitutes and further groups considered undesirable by the 'good' people. To all he expressed the divine pardon and love. By eating with people who were obviously and openly guilty, he received them into God's company. Jesus' claim was clear. Deciding for or against him became tantamount to deciding for or against the divine ruler itself.

What the earthly Jesus *implied* about himself unfolded in the light of the crucifixion and resurrection into the full-blown Christology of the post-Easter Church. It was *not* a movement from a low to a high Christology, as if Jesus made only minimal and modest claims about his personal identity which were later maximized into the high Christology which called him Lord, Son of God and—eventually— God. Rather the shift took place between the implicit Christology of the ministry and the explicit Christology of the emerging Church. Many scholars of all denominations make such an implied Christology one of their major conclusions from a study of Jesus' ministry.

(b) Above I spoke of Jesus being used as 'a principle for criticising the Church'. This phrase masks two related but distinguishable tendencies in contemporary theology. First of all, at every level it has become clear that more and more Church leaders, theologians and other Christians have recognized that ecclesiastical issues will never be resolved unless we push further back—to our understanding of Christ himself. Christology criticises and determines ecclesiology. In its turn our Church theory and practice will condition both what we think about Jesus and how we go about living as his disciples.

Both during and after the Second Vatican Council Schillebeeckx and Küng devoted their theological expertise to the cause of community reform. With prodigal energy Küng wrote about the Church— her past, present and future. Back in 1965 Kasper published his *Dogma unter dem Wort Gottes,* a book that widely influenced thinking on dogmatic formulations. Instinctively all three theologians swung in unison towards the basic Christological issues and in the same year (1974) produced their Jesus-books. Experiences since the closing of the Council have shown that any efforts to renew the Church will remain spiritually empty, emotionally hollow and doctrinally unsound unless they draw inspiration and strength from the Founder of Christianity himself. The Council attended to ecclesiastical problems. It produced a range of documents on the Church, ecumenism, the liturgy, relations with other religions, the roles of bishops, priests, religious and laity, missionary activity and the rest. But it considered Christology only secondarily. If Vatican III were to meet in late 1983, its major document would not be 'The Church in the Modern World' but some response to the question: Who is Jesus Christ for us today? Vawter brought out into the open what many were thinking by insisting on just such a 'priority of Christ' over any ecclesiastical issues.[26]

Second, the historical figure of Jesus can come into play not simply to remind us that ecclesiastical doctrines must be subordinated to Christological beliefs, but to provide grounds for criticising—at times intensely—current Church life. Käsemann in his *Jesus Means Freedom* and elsewhere has underlined that unique freedom which Jesus both gave and demanded. And yet 'freedom', Käsemann reflects, is one of the last words Church leaders wish to hear, let alone use. Boff (*Jesus Christ Liberator*) takes the standpoint of Latin

American theology to maintain that every theology of liberation must establish Jesus as a critical principle *against* the Church. Holl (*Jesus in Bad Company*) sees the challenge of Jesus' ministry in this question: Will society and the Church come to grips with their forgotten minorities and worry less about the 'good', average people?

Küng presses anachronistic language into service and finishes up with a Jesus whose conflicts with Jewish leaders—dare one say it?—prefigure the author's battles with Church authorities. *On Being a Christian* repeatedly speaks of the 'Jewish hierarchy' whose zeal for the 'prevailing dogmas' and 'infallible propositions' brings Jesus down. The political charges before Pilate conceal the 'envy of the hierarchy and its court-theologians'. An 'inquisitorial zeal for the law' prevents the hierarchy from letting 'this radical' go. He is provoking proper authority, represents 'a rebellion against the hierarchy and its theology' and would only cause 'confusion and insecurity'.[27]

How should we assess the current efforts to take the story of Jesus as a basis for criticising the Christian Church? On the one hand, such approaches can go wildly wrong. An interest in Jesus may be used to justify disengagement from the Church, as if one could truly and fully find him apart from the community he called into being. Or else talk about Jesus and his ministry may lapse into feasting on the carrion comfort of abusing Church leaders.

On the other hand, however, the history of Jesus can undoubtedly stand in judgment on the way Christians often live and react. An anecdote from the 1960s illustrates this point better than any argument. A Catholic curate told his bishop how he had arranged an ecumenical service for the boys and girls from the local high school. The arrangement had been made that the non-Catholic students would leave after a bible service, while the Catholics would remain for a Mass. 'But they all stayed', the curate explained, 'and at the time for Holy Communion most of them started coming up to the altar.' 'What did you do?' the bishop asked. 'Well', said the curate, 'I thought to myself, what would Jesus have done?' The bishop broke in aghast: 'You didn't, did you?'

Too often, of course, neither individual Christians nor Christian communities even ask themselves: 'What would Jesus do?' Rather they invoke his name and authority to support religious practices, social standards and political activities that they have *already* endorsed on other grounds. Here none of us have any conscience to examine but our own. But we will find that few methods have greater power to create true sensitivity towards the divine will than regular meditation on episodes from the ministry of Jesus. In that way his ministry can become a principle for deeply criticising our own lives.

(c) Finally, the *language* of Jesus' ministry continues to attract fresh studies. Their findings vary enormously in value. A recent work concluded by announcing that 'Jesus emerges from this study as one whose language must be distinguished from casual speech'! Is this another example of scholars making the obvious look like a great discovery?

One approach which has been monotonously neglected but which seems worth pursuing is the language of Jesus *as a clue to his imagination*. Without presenting us with an exact transcript of the words Jesus used, the synoptic writers (Matthew, Mark and Luke) preserve the flow and flavour of his preaching. This expressive language allows us to glimpse the ways in which his imagination functioned. His eye had scanned a great deal of normal human living. His sensibility betrayed its preferences. He employed, for instance, a large number of farming images but few images drawn from history, geography, warfare and some aspects of home life, for instance the mother-child relationship. There was a hereness and a nowness about the language of Jesus, a preoccupation with the scene right in front of him. In short, the images he used yield some hints about the way he perceived his world.[28]

Let us now conclude this chapter. Our first chapter noted the tendency of traditional theology to separate the person of Christ from his saving 'work', that is to say, Christology from soteriology. This separation divided him into two zones of reality, *who* he was/is and *what* he did/does. In the next chapter we examine how well contemporary theology overcomes this division.

3
Soteriology
and Christology

The first chapter noted how classical theology normally treated the *person* of Jesus Christ apart from his saving *work*. To put this in technical terms, Christology was separated from soteriology. In this chapter we reflect on contemporary attempts to overcome the person-work separation and deal with salvation through Christ.

Functional or Ontological?

When they seek to rehabilitate soteriology, many of the wiser spirits today remark that they do *not* intend to choose a merely functional approach and abandon ontological assertions about Jesus. Kasper dismisses any such 'dilemma' of 'an ontological and a functional Christology' as 'a fictitious problem and an alternative into which theology should not let itself get maneuvered'.[29] Jesus' value and function for us demand that we examine and recognize his status at the level of his being. His saving work indicates both *who* he was and is—both in himself and in his relationship to the Father. There can be no satisfactory account of what Jesus does if we dismiss as unimportant the question who he is. Every soteriological statement has its Christological implications. This point has won wide acceptance and in any case seems obvious enough. To go on insisting that one cannot pursue a functional approach without somehow taking an ontological stand looks like exhuming and beating a thoroughly dead horse.

Nevertheless, some critics of Küng's *On Being a Christian* level the charge that, when he finally comes to discuss Christ's pre-existence, he lapses into a merely functional Christology. The book may offer an unsatisfactory version of pre-existence. But my point here is this. In principle it appears impossible to speak of some person's value, significance and role without making at least some implicit claims about the nature of that person. A merely functional Christology which sets aside ontological issues is simply not feasible. Küng declines to try his hand at such an impossible task. His approach may be 'primarily' functional, but it is not exclusively so.[30]

From Implicit to Explicit Soteriology

Genuine debate has flared up in recent years over the redemptive value that Jesus attached to his coming death. Theoretically, two extremes are possible here. (a) On the one hand, it could be argued that there was no connection at all between what Jesus intended and what actually overtook him. Crucifixion abruptly cut his life short and brought salvation to the human race. But he neither expected nor intended to bring this about. The value of his death in no sense derived from his deliberate purposes. (b) On the other hand, one might assert that Calvary and its effects were totally foreseen by Jesus—right from babyhood. Past versions of that extreme account described his death as premeditated to the extent that they made it look like suicide. Or at any rate his life became cruelly incredible. It was spent under a conscious countdown to death by torture killing. What sense could we make of a man who right from his cradle clearly anticipated and fully accepted a crucifixion which he knew to be fixed for a certain day, hour and place?

Among recent writers Pannenberg has gone as far as any in playing down the voluntary obedience of Jesus. The way he explains matters, Jesus was so seized by his mission that he was scarcely left with any genuinely human choice about accepting or refusing his fate on Calvary.[31] At the other end of the spectrum of opinions, Muggeridge attributes to Jesus a long-range knowledge and acceptance of his execution. Jesus realized from the start that something dreadful waited for him at the end of the road. Yet even Muggeridge pulls back from suggesting that right from the beginning Jesus anticipated and accepted death in the precise form of crucifixion. He writes: 'From the beginning, it had been borne in upon him that the only possible outcome of the mission on earth God had confided to him was an ignominious and *public death.*'[32]

All in all, it is hard to find any contemporary author, whether scholarly or popular, settling clearly for either of the extremes mentioned above. Nevertheless, a fairly recent debate between Hans Kessler, Heinz Schürmann and others exemplifies the trend to either minimalize or maximalize matters. Kessler has pressed the case that the crucifixion was something which overtook Jesus rather than being a destiny which he embraced and interpreted in advance. Schürmann, however, insists that Jesus understood his coming death as the culmination of his mission and—within the circle of his disciples—used his farewell meal to indicate that human salvation would result from his execution.[33]

Any discussion here will only shamble and shuffle along if it fails to distinguish between ascertainable facts and intelligible principles—or, if you like, between historical exegesis and theology. A passage from Vawter's *This Man Jesus* illustrates the way in which an argument can shift from the historical to the theological level:

> Did he [i.e., Jesus] not only foresee his death as a substantive part of his mission, but also cast himself in a role like that of the Servant of the Lord . . . ? It is probably impossible to prove either that he did or did not. . . . The fact that has validated belief in the atoning power of Jesus' death is not the psychology of Jesus, but the atonement itself. . . . The testimony of Christian men who professed their lives to be God's gift through a crucified Saviour thus established the "fact" of vicarious atonement in a way that Jesus' premonition of it *could* [not] or *did* not.[34]

The case here moves from (a) what historians may establish concerning the things Jesus 'foresaw'—his 'psychology' and 'premonitions' about his execution—to (b) what 'could' validate and establish the redemptive value of that death.

To my mind, no version of Calvary delivers a satisfactory form of *theological* goods unless it appreciates how Jesus went knowingly and willingly to his death. If we strike out any genuinely free purpose on his part, we turn him into a passive victim whose murder God picked to serve for the salvation of mankind. Such a version certainly cannot enlist support from the contemporary readiness to recognize how far personal freedom shapes reality. In an essential way subjective intentions affect the meaning of actions. We can only expect that the value of Good Friday was deeply determined by Jesus' own free decision, no less than by the deliberate choices of other men and the freely adopted divine strategy for human salvation. Here one might parody an old principle and say: *Extra libertatem Christi nulla salus.* Theologians should know better than to interpret Calvary in terms of the Father's freedom and our freedom, while making little of Jesus' freedom in consciously dying for certain purposes. Once we acknowledge how much the voluntary quality of the crucifixion matters, we must press on and ask: What did Jesus hope to achieve through his martyrdom? Thus our theological anxiety to respect his freedom brings us to scrutinize the historical evidence.

Here Schürmann and other scholars admit that in trying to recapture Jesus' intentions in the face of death, we may feel we are largely pulling at broken strings. In Mark 10, 45 Jesus seemingly identified himself with the 'Suffering Servant' whose death would atone for human sin: 'The Son of Man came not to be served but to serve, and to give his life as a ransom for many.' But can we treat this verse as reporting the *ipsissima verba*? In particular, do the words 'a ransom for many' come from the historical Jesus himself? The story of the Last Supper promises that the crucifixion will mediate a new covenant between God and the human race: 'This is my blood of the covenant, which is poured out for many' (Mk 14, 24). But how far has the Eucharistic liturgy of the early Church modified what Jesus actually said the night before he died? The doubts raised about these and other texts may trouble us to the point of deciding to contract out of historical debates and settle for some 'safe' view—a theology which leaves aside the intentions of Jesus before his death. However, we need not despair and in this way abandon history for theology. If the *ipsissima verba* of Jesus often elude us, we can be confident of pinning down something of his *ipsissima intentio*.[35]

Violent death was much more than a vague possibility for Jesus. Herod Antipas killed John the Baptist, Jesus' precursor. To preserve law and order in Palestine the Romans took life easily. From some of his Jewish contemporaries Jesus ran into menacing opposition over the content of his preaching and the style of his life. He relativised sacred traditions, broke the sabbath rest to heal people, associated with religious outcasts, showed himself master in the Jerusalem Temple by temporarily assuming authority there—in his own name—interpreted the divine will and communicated the divine pardon. Doubtless the gospels exaggerate the extent of the conflict with the Pharisees, Sadducees and other groups. But it is clear that by the end of Jesus' ministry no major religious and/or political body would step forward to defend him. When he made his journey to Jerusalem and cleansed the Temple, the situation could only have looked extremely threatening. Most readers will find little difficulty in agreeing that—like the prophets before him—Jesus put himself on a deadly collision course through fidelity to his vocation. We may, however, flounder and stagger when faced with the question: What did Jesus *intend to bring about* by accepting the victim-role which was thrust upon him? The evidence seems fugitive right at this decisive point.

Schürmann and others point us in the right direction. They recall attitudes which characterised the ministry of Jesus: service, love and engagement on behalf of sinners. He went about as one who wished to serve all, associated with sinners and offered them God's forgiveness—despite the outrage this caused to 'the righteous'. Geza Vermes sums up this unique feature of Jesus' practice:

> In one respect more than any other he differed from both his contemporaries and even his prophetic predecessors. The prophets spoke on behalf of the honest poor, and defended the widows and the fatherless, those oppressed and exploited by the wicked, rich and powerful. Jesus went further. In addition to proclaiming these blessed, he actually took his stand among the pariahs of his world, those despised by the respectable. Sinners were his table-companions and the ostracised tax-collectors and prostitutes his friends.[36]

The consistent characteristics of Jesus' mission of love converge to suggest his *ipsissima intentio*. He anticipated and accepted death not simply as the consequence of his prophetic mission but as a last service of love. Death was the climax of a ministry during which, as Schillebeeckx insists, *every* action announced, promised and offered salvation.[37]

In these terms the whole ministry yields one major clue to Jesus' attitudes when faced with his violent death. The other major clue comes from the current Jewish idea that a just man could represent others and expiate their sins by dying. This conviction was in the air. It would seem almost unaccountably odd that the vicarious role of his death never occurred to Jesus. He who had shown himself the Servant of all accepted the vocation to become the *Suffering* Servant for all.

These considerations prevent the redemptive message of the Last Supper from coming as a complete surprise. Jesus knew his impending death would atone for the sins of 'many'. Moreover, he linked his fate with the coming rule of God. The liturgy of the early Church simply does not account for one key saying from the Last Supper narrative: 'Truly, I say to you, I shall not drink again of the fruit of the vine until that day when I drink it new in the kingdom of God' (Mk 14, 25). This text takes us right back to Jesus' last meal with his core-group, that 'night before he died.' In brief, the coming rule of God and atonement for sin shaped the *ipsissima intentio* of Jesus—at least during the last days of his ministry.

We can speak of the earthly Jesus' largely *implicit* soteriology which Paul and the early Church developed into an *explicit* soteriology. Brown and other scholars have talked of the implicit Christology of the ministry being succeeded by the explicit Christology of the post-Easter community.[38] This terminology which concerns the *person* of Jesus can be usefully extended to his work. Kasper prefers to contrast a 'hidden soteriology' of Jesus' ministry with the revealed soteriology proclaimed after Pentecost.[39] It seems, however, rather distracting and intrusive to vary terminology here. An implicit/explicit soteriology both matches the popular scheme of an implicit/explicit Christology, and truly expresses the shift from (a) what the preaching of Jesus implied about salvation to (b) what the Holy Spirit led Paul to affirm clearly: Christ 'gave himself for our sins to deliver us from the present evil age' (Gal 1, 4).

The Language of Salvation

Most scholars writing on Jesus Christ show themselves sensitively aware of the need to watch their language and not thoughtlessly slip into adopting current jargon. Did Jesus prove to be a 'revolutionary'? Is the salvation he promised usefully called 'liberation'? Or have revolution and liberation become catch-all terms applied to such a wide variety of phenomena that soteriology can well do without this language?

Küng takes 'revolution' to apply properly to the sudden and violent overthrowing of some social order. He points to the evidence against describing Jesus as a social revolutionary. But then he comes around to allow that Jesus proved to be 'more revolutionary than the revolutionaries'.[40] Others betray nervousness over 'liberation'. Its political connotations may misrepresent the saving message of Jesus. Kasper knows the problems, but he keeps his head, recalls the concern with 'emancipation' that sprang from the Enlightenment,[41] and ends by presenting redemption as 'liberation *(Befreiung)*'.[42]

It would be unfair to belittle the performance of any theologians as they wrestle with the terminology to be used about salvation. Nevertheless, some show themselves heedless of the niceties of language when it comes to dealing with one topic—Christ's precise role. Words like 'representative *(Stellvertreter)*', 'substitute *(Ersatzmann)*' and 'solidarity' continue to be employed in a confused and cumbersome way.

In the 1960s critics took issue with Pannenberg for the carelessness he showed in explaining how Christ was our 'penal substitute'. If someone genuinely represents me, I must agree to his doing so and he must freely undertake the task. Representation is voluntary on both sides, as well as being restricted to specific areas and limited periods of time. A substitute, however, may be simply put in the place of another person or thing. Thus we can substitute a pawn for a castle on a chess-board. Another football player may serve as substitute for a player injured on his way to a match. On the field the substitute takes the place of the injured man, who may be unconscious and hence without knowledge that someone is acting as his substitute. In wartime another prisoner may be shot in place of one who has escaped. There should be no need to pile up further examples to illustrate the point. In the case of substitution between persons, the parties concerned may neither know nor be willing that the substitution is taking place. There is less intentionality and more passivity apparent in the way we use the language of 'substitution'. This consideration alone should win support for speaking of 'Christ our representative' and not of 'Christ our substitute'.

Küng does not take the necessary care about terminology in this area. He moves easily from talking about Christ's *solidarity* and identification with 'sinners of all kinds' to conclude that 'he died as the sinners' representative'—indeed, as mankind's *representative* 'before God'.[43] But what counts as representation here? I can feel deep solidarity with a group of suffering people without being their representative. Conversely, someone can have power of attorney for me, although I feel little solidarity with this legal representative. Küng's usage may not win acquiescence from those schooled to be precise in language.

Kasper also should be more discriminating about such words as 'representative', 'discipleship' and 'solidarity'. He argues that Jesus' 'call to discipleship . . . implied the notion of representation'.[44] This seems wide of the mark. Some 'master' can invite me to be his disciple without undertaking to be my representative before God and man. No one that I have met considers himself to be a disciple of his legal representative, although some people take that attitude toward their political representatives. In general, discipleship and representation do not necessarily imply each other. Doubtless the disciples of Jesus enjoyed a degree of solidarity with the master who invited them to follow him. One can also admit that it belonged to this discipleship that he did 'something "for us" '.[45] But more evidence is required to show that *as such* 'the call to discipleship'—at least in the case of Jesus—implied 'the notion of representation'. He said to Simon and Andrew: 'Follow me and I will make you become fishers of men' (Mk 1, 17). The call to discipleship did not take the form of saying or implying: 'Follow me and I will become your saving representative before my Father in dying to expiate your sins'. When the language of expiation surfaces later, Mark has Jesus speak of giving his life 'as a ransom for many' (10, 45), and not just as a ransom for the disciples with him. Of course, one might simply identify Jesus' disciples with all those saved through his representative death and resurrection. In that case the call to discipleship would coincide with a call to salvation as such and hence imply representation. The commission to 'make disciples of all nations' (Mt 28, 19) could encourage us to adopt this broad notion of discipleship. But in that case we must cease thinking of discipleship as entailing some special generosity which only a small minority can muster—a sentiment to which Thomas à Kempis gave classic expression:

> Jesus has now many lovers of his heavenly kingdom, but few bearers of his cross. . . . He finds many companions of his table, but few of his abstinence. . . . All desire to rejoice with him, but few are willing to endure anything for his sake. Many follow Jesus to the breaking of bread, but few to the drinking of the chalice of his passion (Bk II, ch. 11).

In dealing with soteriological language, I believe it only right to mention a recent effort to rehabilitate the language of *satisfaction* which St. Anselm's *Cur Deus Homo* gave to Christian theology. Anselm (c. 1033-1109) was the first writer to devote a treatise explicitly to the atonement. His soteriology won wide endorsement from theologians in the Middle Ages, during the Reformation and later. Although few go as far as Adolf von Harnack ('no theory so bad had ever before his day been given out as ecclesiastical'), some twentieth-century scholars have dismissed talk of satisfaction as foreign to contemporary insights and treated Anselm himself as little more than an interesting survivor from a theological disaster area. It became customary to label his theory as Roman, legalistic and engrossed with the divine honour rather than the divine love.

However, John McIntyre, Gispert Greshake and now Walter Kasper have argued for the subtlety and splendour of Anselm's theology of satisfaction. This version of the atonement appreciates God's *fidelity* to creation and the moral order in a way that parallels

St. Paul's sense of divine 'righteousness' (Rom 1, 17 etc.). Taken within the feudal context, the divine honour implies rather than excludes love. For Anselm 'honour' guarantees peace, order and justice. Lastly, his view of the atonement reflects the Germanic rather than the Roman culture and customs. Kasper has shown himself favourable to this fresh estimate of *Cur Deus Homo*.[46] But Küng, his colleague at the University of Tübingen, repeats the well-worn criticisms of Anselm's theology of satisfaction.[47]

Salvation from What?

Kasper and Küng also differ as regards the lostness from which Christ's saving work delivers men and women. Both take time out to ask in depth: What keeps the questions of salvation and redemption alive today? Both recognise evil as that present reality and profound mystery from which we yearn to be saved. Evil includes human sin but goes beyond it. (In parentheses we can note how the pair from Tübingen prove here much superior to Pannenberg. He cannot really handle soteriology because he has not sufficiently faced the problem of evil. Pannenberg has frankly admitted this gap in his theology: 'The role played by sin, evil, suffering, destruction and brokenness in human history has not received very extensive treatment in my writings.'[48]) Where Kasper and Küng pull apart is over the setting in which they choose to talk about human liberation from evil.

Kasper quickly informs his readers that 'the crisis of meaning in modern society' is 'the place where Christology becomes relevant beyond the narrow context of theology'. The background to this crisis he traces through a list of German writers: Novalis, Fichte, Schelling, Hegel, Nietzsche and Heidegger. These and other authors indicate the way meaningless nihilism has come to threaten us.[49] Here Kasper takes a very European attitude towards the lostness from which Christ promises to rescue us. At least at this point he bypasses the demonic 'crises' produced by hunger, drugs, corrupt government, new forms of international exploitation, exploding cities, the systematic use of torture, massacres in Cambodia, civil war in Lebanon, and all the other horrors perpetrated by human fear and greed. To be sure, Kasper gives 'liberation' a key place in his soteriology and rightly remarks that any discussion of Jesus Christ must try to relate 'a Christian understanding of redemption and a modern understanding of emancipation'.[50] Nevertheless, he writes for North Atlantic readers or—more accurately—for Europeans who hunger for meaning but find a banal world without and an emptiness within.[51] Kasper fails to reflect on the questions of salvation, the crisis of meaning and the sense of lostness which might be alive today in Africa, India, Latin America, and the New China after Mao Tse-tung. Or are we to suppose that the 'crisis of meaning' in contemporary Europe is paradigmatic for the rest of the world?

Küng does better. At the outset his eye runs from Leningrad to Tashkent, to New Delhi and Bangkok and then on to Tokyo and Melbourne.[52] He then gives his interpretation of Christianity and Christ a wide context which embraces Hinduism and other major religions, various forms of Marxism and that whole world which modern technology is fashioning almost everywhere. At times Küng's comments may leave some readers outraged. Thus he takes up Jesus' 'good news to the poor', observes that 'everyman' meets 'the temptation to live by bread alone', and insists that Jesus preached 'to the damned of this world' that 'beyond the satisfying of economic needs they are—in a much deeper sense—poor, miserable, exploited and needy'.[53] If I am well-fed, well-housed and well-clothed, should I tell my starving brothers that Jesus warned us against the temptation to live by bread alone? Nevertheless, one can only applaud Küng's thoroughgoing attempt to situate his Christology, soteriology and whole account of Christian life within a world context. *On Being a Christian* sees him truly moving beyond the narrow horizons of 'mere' Church reform to present Jesus' challenge to universal human aspirations.

Küng takes a broad scale and chooses world guidelines in pursuing his intention to 'activate the memory of Jesus as the one who is *ultimately normative*'.[54] He wants to show that his first-century life, death and resurrection possesses a unique and universal value for human salvation. All the same, one may wonder whether he actually succeeds in producing satisfactory grounds for making such an absolute claim for Jesus. Küng seems to rest much of his case on a repeated contrast between Jesus and the founders of other religious movements. Set alongside Buddha, Mohammed, Moses and Confucius (who is consistently and correctly called Kung-futse), Jesus looks quite different.

> He was not educated at court, as Moses apparently was. He was no son of a king like Buddha. Also he was no scholar and politician like Kung-futse, nor was he a rich merchant like Mohammed. Precisely because his origin was so insignificant, his lasting importance is so astonishing.[55]

Whether we look at Jesus' background, career, message or influence, he evades any comparison.

> None of the great founders of religions worked in so narrow a field. None lived such an outrageously short time. None died so young. And yet what an effect [he had]! Every fourth human being, about a thousand million persons are called Christian. Numerically Christianity comes by a wide margin at the head of all world religions.[56]

Küng marshals expertly the historical data which make Jesus' person and influence appear startlingly different. But does he manage to get beyond facts to the level of *principle*? Millions of people believe Jesus to be 'ultimately normative' for their lives. But what justifies their faith? Historical research gives Küng a stick with which to beat those who would glibly line Jesus up with a standard set of religious figures who have shaped world history. However, does Jesus differ from Buddha, Mohammed, Moses and the rest not merely *de facto*, but also *de iure*? Do we face simply a difference of degree but not one of kind?

   I take it that these comparisons function *apologetically*. They prepare readers to move beyond the historical phenomena to accept in faith the *theological* basis for seeing Jesus as ultimately normative. That basis Küng locates, as Pannenberg and others do, in the events of Good Friday and Easter Sunday. The resurrection puts an absolute stamp of divine approval on the life of Jesus. Despite the shameful crucifixion, the cause of Jesus turns out to be truly the cause of God. Deciding for or against Jesus is nothing less than deciding for or against God. The crucified and risen Jesus personifies the final divine commitment to the world. He offers a definitive answer to the ultimate issues of life, including the questions of suffering and death.[57]

So far this chapter has been sampling contemporary reflections on the redemptive 'work' of Jesus Christ. For the most part it has been a matter of raising questions rather than presenting developed conclusions. One vast theme has been barely touched upon—the nature of salvation. Küng urges that 'being saved' is nothing other than being radically and genuinely human. In *Jesus* Schillebeeckx uses the traditional terminology of 'salvation', suggests that it amounts to what we mean by 'humanisation', and promises to write a soteriology for our times. This is clearly an urgent task. Those who seek to reunite Christology with soteriology will prove successful only if they confront the serious and decisive problems buried in the word 'salvation'. How does one explain today what Jesus Christ saves us for?

In *Christ* (New York, 1980), the second volume of his huge trilogy, Schillebeeckx has produced just such a modern soteriology. Admittedly, much of the book simply reports ways in which the New Testament Christians experienced and interpreted salvation through Christ. Yet the key theme seems sound: redemption comes to human beings who experience the mystery of suffering.

4
Three Contemporary Christologies

So far this book has used six themes to map recent shifts and new emphases in the understanding of Jesus Christ's person and redemptive work. To complement that thematic approach I want now to examine closely three contemporary theologians: James Mackey, Jon Sobrino and Edward Schillebeeckx. All of them built their Christologies out of the story of Jesus' ministry and death. Although they wrote several years later, curiously enough neither Mackey (in 1979) nor Sobrino (in 1978) took notice of Schillebeeckx's attempt (in 1974) to approach Christology through the historical Jesus.

(1) Among more recent Christologies Mackey's *Jesus the Man and the Myth* (New York: Paulist, 1979) has to be the most readable. Its verve and imagination are striking. A deep religious concern and enthusiasm for the cause of Jesus make sections of Mackey's book compelling reading. In offering some comments, I want to relate my remarks to the scheme of six themes given above—taking them in this order: four, five, six and then back to two.

Myth

In his Christology Mackey makes 'myth' a key word (see number four in my list). Unlike the authors of *The Myth of God Incarnate* (of which more later), he explains and handles the term with consistency. Symbols are images which evoke deep and universal experiences. When you weave images and symbols into a story, you have myth. In general myth serves as a perennial way of telling the truth

(p. 36). As regards historical truth, Mackey reasonably argues that myth and history should not be contrasted as if they were mutually exclusive (pp. 33f.). Myth can deal with the historically 'real just as easily as it can deal in the purely fictional' (p. 248). Not only my Irish ancestors bear that out but also a decade of living in Rome. The reunification of Italy ('Il Risorgimento') and the resistance during the Second World War ('La Resistenza') certainly happened, but they have a mythical life of their own which goes far beyond 'mere' history.

All that said, I retain serious doubts about 'myth' in this context. Mackey himself is aware of the practical difficulty in using the word. For the non-scholarly public (to which he primarily addresses his book) 'myth' almost automatically suggests what is unreal and downright false. Moreover, Mackey's account of myth—'a symbol or a series of symbols developed in the form of a *story*' (p. 78; italics mine)—makes me wonder whether his book could better have been called *Jesus the Man and the Story*. The title would then have lacked an attention-grabbing word. Yet does Mackey's book finally do anything else than study Jesus from the viewpoints of history and the profoundly significant story Christians told about him (= their briefer proclamation and fuller doctrine)? The Christological titles can be described as 'building the Jesus myth' (pp. 195–204), but they could be more helpfully seen as a major part of the total story through which early Christians confessed their faith in the crucified and risen Jesus. Mackey deals with the Nicene Creed and later fourth-century accounts of Christ's divinity as 'the full-grown myth' (pp. 210–240). It would be better to speak of the fully developed (and deeply significant) Christian story and doctrine.

The Ministry of Jesus

Apropos of the ministry of Jesus (number five in the themes I discussed above), Mackey rightly maintains that there are no serious *historical* problems about knowing the earthly Jesus. Difficulties normally arise from philosophical preconceptions or from certain theological presuppositions about the link between history and faith. (In the context of the resurrection I want to come back to the issue of Christian faith.)

Mackey beautifully presents some major themes from the public life of Jesus: the kingdom of God, the parables of the kingdom, meals and prayer. He has little to say about that striking feature of the ministry—Jesus' extraordinary claim to *authority* and clear conviction that the divine rule had powerfully come in connection with his person and work. Mackey does not consider the evidence that in his experience of the Father Jesus knew himself to be Son in a unique way. The *faith of Jesus* comes through as the distinguishing feature not only of Chapter IV ('The Life of Jesus') but also of Mackey's whole Christology. Jesus' 'distinctive faith-conviction' (p. 187)—indeed, 'unique faith' (p. 232)—is crucial for Mackey's case that '*only* in Jesus do we meet the one, true God' (p. 264; italics mine).

To begin with, let me say that I believe Mackey to be right in holding that the earthly Jesus had faith. (In my own forthcoming Christology I argue that Jesus' immediate awareness of the divine reality modified his faith as *confession* but left room for faith as *commitment* and *confidence*.) Mackey notes two Catholic authors who have recognized faith in the historical Jesus (p. 296, n. 52), but misses H. Urs von Balthasar and others who should have been added to that list. Mackey correctly appeals to Hebrews for support, but cites 12, 2 as calling Jesus 'the pioneer and perfecter of *our* faith' (p. 168; italics mine). Here theological presuppositions lead practically all English translations (JB, NAB, NIV, RSV; less clearly NEB) to insert 'our', a word which does not appear in the original Greek text. Mackey could have made the point that the whole section in Hebrews on the heroes and heroines of faith (11, 1ff.) climaxes with Jesus. He shows us the perfect example of faith, as he began and completed *his own* life of faith by moving through suffering to the divine joy of the resurrection.

My main difficulties, however, concern Mackey's description of faith and use of Paul. 'Faith' gets reduced to a quite general 'perception/evaluation/acceptance of all life and existence, as gift' (p. 165), which Mackey then properly calls a 'radically human down-to-earth *creation* faith' (p. 211; italics mine). This is a faith which stops short with the first part of the Creed ('I believe in God, the Father almighty, creator of heaven and earth')—a lived conviction and commitment to the God of creation immediately present as Father in our contingent lives. This is an incomplete version of faith which fails to include the elements of eschatological *confidence* (about the future) and, in particular, the *confession* of God's historical acts (in the past). It slides over the confessions of faith to be found both in the Old Testament (for example, Deut 26, 5ff.) and in the New Testament. For Paul, Christian faith involves as an essential element believing that God has raised Jesus from the dead (Rom 10, 9; 1 Cor 15, 1–11). In short, Mackey's account of Christian faith is true but radically insufficient.

Even though he is aware that Paul has very little indeed to say about the life of Jesus (p. 175), nevertheless Mackey maintains that Paul proposes to his readers a life 'lived by the same faith by which Jesus lived' (p. 181). Apropos of prayer, meal-fellowship, service, life, grace, *faith* and spirit, Paul is alleged to 'give us clearly to understand that these features were introduced to our lives by Jesus, that they were features of Jesus' own existence and were caught by us in the contagion of his life-service to our human destiny' (p. 184). But where on earth does Paul 'give us clearly to understand' all that about the life and influence of the earthly Jesus? Mackey makes much of a grammatical possibility offered by Galatians 2, 16 (pp. 163, 188)—namely that we are justified not through believing *in* Jesus Christ (as object of our faith) but through (being infected by) the faith *of* Jesus (the personal subject of his own faith). Mackey has ignored the priority of context over mere grammar. In the context it is clear that Paul is writing of *our* faith *in* Jesus Christ. Every contemporary translation I have checked (JB, NAB, NEB, NIV and RSV) takes the passage in that sense. So too do commentators like H.D. Betz, *Galatians* (Philadelphia: Fortress, 1979), pp. 115–119.

The material on Jesus recorded by Matthew, Mark and Luke offers solid grounds for concluding that the earthly Jesus can rightly be called a believer. Why then does Mackey misuse Paul in the way I have just noted? It seems that by one-sidedly maximizing the life and faith of Jesus, Mackey is committed to showing *a perfect continuity* between the situation of Jesus and that of Paul. Even if Paul uses 'his own conceptual symbols for the new existence of the followers of Jesus' (p. 184), he conveys exactly 'the same sense' as Jesus did through his myth of God's kingdom (p. 177). The crucifixion and resurrection, in Mackey's view, did not essentially change the situation in the divine-human relationship. This is a thesis which is, among other things, simply incompatible with Paul's theology.

Soteriology

Mackey brings together Christology and soteriology (number six in my list of themes), showing how the classic symbols of redemption relate to deep and universal human concerns (pp. 73–85). He is properly alert to the fact that his own particular experience of evil will prove significant, even decisive, for his interpretation of salvation (see, for example, pp. 56, 59, 72).

Certainly Mackey makes absolute claims for Jesus' saving work: 'The radical faith of Jesus . . . *alone* brings us into contact with the God who is truly Father of all' (p. 223; italics mine); '*only* in Jesus does one encounter the one, true God' (p. 233; italics mine; see also p. 264). At the end of the day, however, what Jesus does for us (*pro nobis*) edges out who and what Jesus was/is in himself (*in se*). In effect, Mackey overcomes any separation between Christology and soteriology by having the latter swallow up the former. For example, he tells us:

> The New Testament writers on resurrection are not so much interested in the fact that Jesus of Nazareth lived again by God's act after he had died, and not so much interested in the fact that he was individually translated to a new form of existence [= Christology], as they are interested in depicting a new, dynamic role which he plays in what they believe to be the divine direction of our history in this universe [= soteriology] (p. 194).

This brings me to the most important theme—the resurrection of Jesus.

The Resurrection of Jesus

Many contemporary Christologies center on the resurrection of the crucified Jesus (number two in my list of themes). Mackey, however, focuses primarily on the life and death of Jesus. He doubts whether the resurrection added anything over and above that life and death (pp. 115, 119f.). He finds the light of revelation and the call to faith already there in the ministry of Jesus. The myth of redemption attached itself to the crucifixion. At times Mackey's language drastically devalues the resurrection of Jesus and our own coming resurrection. Yet mere 'survival' after death (see, for example, pp. 114, 120) in no way expressed what Paul in 1 Corinthians 15 and other New Testament authors understand by resurrection. Elsewhere Mackey speaks more accurately of a 'glorious future' beyond death (p. 99; see also pp. 105, 139).

Mackey's general approach to the resurrection should put one's hermeneutical nerves on red alert. He repeatedly asks his readers to put aside 'preconceived notions' (p. 87), to 'rid' their minds 'entirely' of various 'preconceptions' (which he tabulates), and to 'see' the New Testament 'with clear and unblinkered eyes' (pp. 93f.). With a 'clean eye' (p. 109) one will be able to consider 'carefully, comprehensively and without presuppositions' what the Gospels and Paul have to say about the resurrection of Jesus (p. 110). Mackey is particularly hard on those 'propagandist or apologetic' preconceptions (p. 93) which he entitles 'role-requirements' (pp. 87–94)—a priori expectations about the (revealing and redemptive) roles played by the resurrection of Jesus. (Surely we are dealing rather with 'role-*recognition*'—that is to say, with a recognition of the roles Jesus' resurrection did and does play? Later on Mackey himself in a guarded and qualified fashion admits this point [pp. 114ff.])

Here I can only imagine what Hans-Georg Gadamer, Bernard Lonergan and other philosophers would say about the call to rid ourselves of all preconceptions and read the New Testament texts with a 'clean eye'. Such an attempt to imitate once again Descartes' decision to make a totally fresh start is neither necessary nor possible. We should try as much as we can to be aware of our presuppositions and expectations, but we cannot and need not 'rid' ourselves of them 'entirely'. As regards the life of Jesus, Mackey himself makes this very point (p. 291, n. 1). When he comes to the resurrection, does he lapse into a Cartesian-style approach because he is anxious that his readers agree with him? Are those who fail to do so 'blinkered' and suffering from 'preconceived notions' or 'propagandist' and 'apologetic' preconceptions?

I must confess to feeling slightly disenchanted by Mackey's tendency to parody positions he wishes to reject. Those who rightly maintain the priority of Jesus' personal resurrection (of this more later) can only be dismayed to find Mackey apparently describing this as 'the revivification of a corpse' (p. 111), 'the revivification of a dead man' (p. 112), the 'revival of a dead man' (p. 113), and even 'a revived corpse escaping from a tomb' (p. 108)—that is to say, Jesus as 'known to have been revived after death' (p. 110; see also p. 195). There is more than hint here of Rudolf Bultmann's parody of the resurrection (in 'New Testament and Mythology') as an alleged 'miraculous proof' in "the shape of the resuscitation of a dead person".[57a] Both Mackey (at least in the passages quoted above) and Bultmann ignore the *transformation* involved in Jesus' resurrection. It was no mere revivification of a corpse. Earlier in fact Mackey distinguishes this resurrection from the resuscitation/revivification and return to ordinary life of a dead Lazarus (p. 92).

In the discussion of 1 Corinthians 15 the same kind of parody technique turns up—this time as the possibility of understanding the resurrection as a 'proof-miracle' (pp. 96f.). Of course, past apologists have wrongly represented the resurrection in those terms. Mackey has no difficulty in knocking down that particular Aunt Sally, and then quickly allows himself to conclude that St. Paul did *not* understand 'the resurrection of Jesus *primarily* as an event of Jesus' own destiny' (p. 97; italics mine). En route to that conclusion Mackey correctly notes that already as a Pharisee Paul believed that the dead would be raised, but ignores the way in which the apostle's encounter with the risen Jesus changed that belief (p. 96). Pharisees looked for a *general* resurrection at the end of history. Now Paul learned that one person had been raised in anticipation of that end and was the agent through whom all others would be raised (1 Cor 15, 22).

Again and again Paul is not accurately reported. Take this passage, for example:

In some texts the phrase 'the resurrection of Jesus' or 'Jesus is raised' is *aligned with* Paul's experience of his own call to and practice of apostleship. In other words, Paul's vocation and drive to apostleship and the resurrection of Jesus *refer to the same experience* in his [Paul's] life. 'Am I not an apostle?' he asks the Corinthians. 'Have I not seen Jesus our Lord?' (p. 100; italics mine).

'Aligned with' is a vague phrase. One might, however, charitably agree to use it of Galatians 1. There Paul first writes of 'God the Father' who raised Jesus Christ from the dead (1, 1), and then tells us that the risen Christ was revealed to him (Paul)—a revelation which constituted a call to preach the good news to the Gentiles (1, 12.16). Encountering the risen Christ coincided with the call to faith and apostolic ministry. But it baffles me how Mackey can add that 'Paul's vocation' and 'the resurrection of Jesus refer to the same experience' in Paul's life. The opening chapter of Galatians tells a different story. First, the Father raised Jesus from the dead; Paul for some time persecuted the young Church; only then did the revelation of the risen Son give Paul his Christian vocation. Further, Mackey glosses over the fact that in the verse he quotes (1 Cor 9, 1) Paul does *not* ask 'Am I not an apostle? Have I not seen *the resurrection*?' Instead Paul recalls his vision of the (already) risen Jesus as the legitimation of his apostolic ministry.

Another example. Mackey reports that 'for Paul, to say that Jesus is risen *is* to say that Jesus is the Lord or the Spirit in his life and in the lives of his converts' (p. 104; italics mine; see also pp. 97, 99). As so often, such an 'is-statement' remains ambiguous. It would be more accurate and acceptable if we unpack it as follows: The resurrection of Jesus (= A) has caused and brought about his Lordship in the life of Paul and others (= B). Undoubtedly, for Paul (A) is unthinkable unless it is followed by (B). But (A) is not identical with—it is not the same event as—(B).

Mackey assures us that Jesus' special appearance to him is not as such important to Paul. *'The only thing'* the apostle wants us to understand about 'this pivotal experience' is that 'it was his conversion to the one and only gospel that came from Jesus himself, the one good news which, when we allow it to form in us the faith that guides our lives, is the very power of God himself to save us'. Hence Mackey concludes that 'the appearance of the risen Jesus' to Paul 'comes down to his reception of the gospel' (p. 103; italics mine). I am afraid all this invites the comment: 'The appearance of Jesus is swallowed up in Paul's conversion. O appearance, where is thy victory? O appearance, where is thy sting?'

To establish his case against the importance of the risen Lord's special appearance to the apostle, Mackey introduces an argument from silence. Paul gives us no 'detailed description of the one who appeared, and of how he made himself known, of the circumstances of the appearances, and of what, in particular, was said or otherwise communicated'. When, however, 'something of importance needed to be said or insisted upon', Paul 'was never noticeably short of words or images or ideas' (p. 103).

I wonder. On any showing, the *crucifixion* of Jesus was extremely important to Paul. Yet the apostle provides no details whatsoever of its circumstances. From his letters we hear nothing about the arrest, the trial(s), the scourging, the crowning with thorns, and such central figures as Judas, Caiaphas and Pilate.[57b] Paul does not even mention Jerusalem as the scene of the crucifixion. Everything gets swallowed up in the simple affirmation that Jesus was crucified for us (1 Cor 1, 13). Once Paul has exclaimed with astonishment, 'The Son of God loved me and gave himself for me' (Gal 2, 20), he has really said all he wishes to say. Something like this happens with the resurrection and (part of) its aftermath, that truly 'pivotal experience' when 'last of all' Jesus 'appeared also to me' (1 Cor 15, 8). Once Paul has recalled that Christ was raised and, after appearances to others, appeared also to the great persecutor and made him an apostle (1 Cor 15, 4–9), Paul has said all that he wishes to say.

In Mackey's interpretation, Paul's conversion and reception of the good news become an experience which only chronologically precedes that of later Christians but does not differ from the possibilities open to them. At any time in the history of Christianity people can allow themselves to be formed in exactly the same way by 'the one and only gospel'. We are dealing here with 'a myth the truth of which can be tested by any followers of Jesus, from the follower so powerfully inspired as to become a missionary, to the one who has barely touched its energy field' (p. 120). This myth of the resurrection, according to Mackey, conveys the conviction that 'the effect' of 'an act of God on and through Jesus . . . was, or could be, contemporary *with anyone* who heard the myth proclaimed in any acceptable form *at any time*' (p. 258; italics mine). As Mackey interprets the record, the risen Jesus did not produce different 'effects'—appearing to some and making them the original witnesses (those who 'saw and believed'), and through the testimony of these witnesses calling others to Easter-faith (those who 'do not see and yet believe').

If we agree with Mackey that Paul and the other apostles did not have—and therefore cannot witness to—a *special experience* of the risen Christ, there seems to be no reason for maintaining their special, non-transferable and non-repeatable functions as mediators of foundational revelation and founders of the Church. Mackey's position on the Easter appearances carries serious consequences for the theology of revelation and the Church. Here he stands apart from Küng, Rahner and Sobrino, who all rightly defend the *special* nature and importance of the risen Christ's appearances to Peter, Paul and the other apostolic witnesses. (On this see further my *Fundamental Theology* [Ramsey, N.J.: Paulist, 1981], pp. 89–91, 99, 101f., 235f., 261f., and *What Are They Saying about the Resurrection?* [New York: Paulist, 1978], pp. 58–60.)

Behind Mackey's view of the resurrection is his theology of *faith*. In the making of faith he does not care for 'evidence' provided by the past (pp. 99, 103, 112). Specifically, 'we have in the New Testament no evidence offered us which was ever of *an objectively verifiable kind* and which could *prove* the personal resurrection of Jesus' (p. 286; see p. 261). This is a statement which cries out for some distinctions. Certainly the New Testament offers us no *merely* objectively verifiable evidence which could *by itself* strictly prove the personal resurrection of Jesus. Neither apropos of the resurrection nor of anything else does the New Testament propose merely scientific, neutral evidence which could alone publicly demonstrate to disengaged observers that such and such was (or continues to be) the case. What the New Testament essentially witnesses to will be accepted by those who freely let themselves be opened up subjectively and become hearers of the word. Nevertheless, that is not at all to deny that the New Testament offers historical evidence and signs pointing to Jesus' personal resurrection, above all the credible witness of apostles like Peter and Paul. Of course, there is no 'coercive evidence for the personal resurrection of the man Jesus' (pp. 262f.). Here, as elsewhere, properly 'coercive' evidence would rule out faith, which is always free. But the absence of 'coercive' evidence is *not* the same as the absence of *all* evidence. The absence of 'clear and cogent circumstantial evidence' (p. 194) is simply not equivalent to the absence of all evidence. In any case, who decides here what counts as 'clear and cogent circumstantial evidence'? A resolute skeptic like David Hume would in principle never allow even the greatest amount of evidence to count against our common experience that dead men do not rise. (On Hume see my *The Resurrection of Jesus Christ* [Valley Forge: Judson, 1973], pp. 67f.)

What Mackey has done is to downplay the role of reasonable evidence from the past and maximize what he calls the present 'experiential counterpart' (pp. 115, 117, 120) in the making of (Easter) faith. *Our experience now* becomes the decisive (p. 117), even (with the help of the Holy Spirit) the only, factor in establishing and maintaining faith: 'The experience' of Jesus' power in our lives 'can *alone* convince us today that Jesus lives and reigns' (p. 112; italics mine). Back in 1973 in Chapter VI of *The Resurrection of Jesus Christ,* I argued that the present 'existential correlate' *and* the historical witness/evidence from the past converge to make and justify Easter faith. I am still utterly convinced that we are dealing here with a 'both/and'—rather than an 'either/or'—situation.

Finally, Mackey denies neither the personal resurrection of Jesus nor the final resurrection we hope for. But he privileges excessively 'all that we can experience and therefore really understand of Jesus as a spirit or power in our present lives' (p. 105; see p. 117). Undoubtedly Mackey is right in counterbalancing any versions of the resurrection which would minimize its *present* powerful values and concentrate either on the *past* resurrection of Jesus or our own *future* resurrection. I have to agree with Mackey over that, as in 1978 I made the same point in my *What Are They Saying about the Resurrection?* (pp. 18–24). Yet this is no justification for overemphasizing the present and declining to hold the past, present and future together in a dynamic synthesis. Mackey speaks of himself as 'juggling tenses' and showing 'disregard for the distinction between past and present tenses' (p. 258). It would be more accurate to say that the past is collapsed into the present and that consistently the present is one-sidedly privileged.

(2) Spanish-born Jon Sobrino certainly does not exaggerate when he observes that the theological milieu of an author is highly significant (pp. 18f.). He himself teaches at the University of José Simeón Cañas of El Salvador. Originally published in Spanish (1976), his *Christology at the Crossroads* came out in English as a revised and enlarged edition (Maryknoll, N.Y.: Orbis, 1978). Sobrino has survived several attempts on his life. When he writes of Jesus dying 'as a direct result of historical sin' (pp. xvif.), the same thing might have happened to Sobrino. The situation in which he wrote and practices his Christology puts it and Sobrino himself in a class quite apart from the other contemporary authors I discuss in this book. None of them has freely continued to risk paying such a high price for commitment to Jesus and his cause—a point to which I will return later.

Sobrino and Mackey

(a) To introduce *Christology at the Crossroads* I want to compare and contrast it with Mackey's work. Unlike Mackey, Sobrino has a low doctrine of *symbol* and *myth*. The index gives only one reference to 'myth' (p. 271, n. 5) and nothing under 'symbol'. Sobrino frankly aims at breaking 'the inertia of more mythical thinking about Jesus' (p. 80), overcoming 'the aura of mythology that surrounds Christology' (p. 79), and getting back to the real historical Jesus.

Whatever we say about the category of 'myth', Sobrino suffers through disregarding and downgrading symbols. He contrasts 'symbolic expression' with 'concrete reality' (p. 348), forgetting that those images which evoke deep experiences can be as historically 'concrete' as one could ever wish. One needs only to recall a scene from San Salvador itself in March 1980: Oscar Romero gunned down at the altar like a latter-day St. Thomas Becket. The blood on the archbishop's vestments reminds me of a specific omission in the area of symbolism: Sobrino remains uneasy about invoking the *expiatory* model of redemption and its language of *blood*. He mentions Christ's blood only three times in the whole book (pp. 189, 262, 303). But, of course, many other theologians today make little of expiation, and some translations of the New Testament in places 'suppress' Christ's blood. (See my "Our Peace and Reconciliation," *The Way* 22 [1982], pp. 112–21, at p. 113.)

Mackey's sound appreciation of symbolic language shows up clearly when he deals with the end of history and the coming reign of God. As he points out, it is a mistake to interpret Jesus' prophetic-apocalyptic teaching about the 'end' literalistically and in terms of linear time (pp. 127f., 292, n. 8). Sobrino, however, although he helpfully reflects on the element of genuine futurity involved in that teaching (pp. 355f.), should have attended to the symbolic nature of Jesus' language. That would have stopped him from making such an unqualified assertion: 'Jesus expected the imminent end of history, the imminent arrival of God's kingdom' (p. 306; see also pp. 134, 389).

(b) Like Mackey, Sobrino centers his Christology on Jesus' *ministry and death* and develops the theme of Jesus' faith. Unlike Mackey, however, Sobrino has more to say about Jesus' practice of and teaching on prayer (pp. 146–78), argues that Jesus' way of acting and speaking implied a distinctive consciousness regarding not only his mission for the kingdom but also his unique and exclusive relationship to the Father (pp. 67–74), sets out more fully the evidence for Jesus' faith provided by the Synoptic Gospels (Chapter IV), notes a range of Catholic theologians who have recognized the faith exercised by the earthly Jesus (p. 139, n. 3), and maintains that at some point in the ministry an important change of perspective took place—a shift from Jesus' initial faith to his final, definitive faith (pp. 92ff.).

Undoubtedly there are details to be challenged in the way Sobrino presents the last point—the 'rupture' in Jesus' faith. What real evidence, for example, supports the claim that Jesus was 'tempted to withdraw into seclusion, to picture his mission more in terms of some restricted sect' (p. 94)? Nevertheless, the general point appears true. At some stage circumstances led Jesus to modify his intentions and expectations. He willingly shifted from 'a love embodied in effective action to a love embodied in suffering' (p. 135). As we shall, the Papal Theological Commission also endorsed some kind of shift of perspective on the part of Jesus. My own *The Calvary Christ* (Philadelphia: Westminster, 1977) followed Schoonenberg in arguing for the same point (pp. 26ff.).

Like Mackey, incidentally, Sobrino (p. 88) seems unaware that the original Greek of Hebrews 12, 2 does not call Jesus 'the pioneer and perfecter of *our* faith' but 'the pioneer and perfecter of faith'—in the context, *his own* faith. Sobrino comments: 'The text asserts that Jesus is the one who initiates *their* faith and brings it to perfection' (p. 89; italics mine). Later, however, he describes Jesus' faith in terms which make a splendidly accurate paraphrase of Hebrews 12, 2: 'Jesus is the one who has lived faith in all its pristine fullness, who has opened up the pathway of faith and traversed it to the very end' (p. 107).

(c) Striking differences emerge between Sobrino and Mackey when we come to the resurrection. Unlike Mackey, Sobrino acknowledges *the radical change* brought by the resurrection—'the definitive historical action of God' and hence 'a new historical definition of God' (pp. 182f.; see p. 377). 'In the resurrection of the crucified one' Christian faith had 'its origin' (p. 184). Sobrino is clear about the *special nature* of the risen Christ's appearance: 'There can be no historical doubt that the disciples had some sort of privileged experience' (p. 375).

(d) Finally, Sobrino dramatically differs from Mackey in *not privileging present experience*. He interprets the resurrection 'in terms of a promise that opens up a future' (p. 253). Although Sobrino agrees that 'the resurrection is laid hold of not only in hopeful expectation for the end of history' but also 'in here-and-now love', at once he adds that 'amid the concrete conditions of present history' this love 'anticipates what is promised in the resurrection' (p. 255).

In general, Sobrino argues that all Christological reflection 'must be oriented toward the future of history'. He privileges that future horizon rather than past or present experience: 'Jesus' past can be recovered in the present *only if* it pushes us toward the future' (p. xxiii; italics mine).

The Starting Point of Christology?

Sobrino is obviously right in holding that 'there can be no Christology of Christ apart from the history of Jesus of Nazareth' (p. xii; see point five in my list of themes). In the next chapter we will see how the Theological Commission firmly endorsed the place of Jesus' ministry in any adequate Christology.

Sobrino, however, goes further. He takes as the starting point and, in fact, the center of his Christology the historical Jesus—that is to say, 'the person, proclamation, activity, attitudes, and death by crucifixion of Jesus of Nazareth insofar as all of this can be gathered from the New Testament texts' (p. 351). Sobrino aims to present the 'traits of Jesus which are most securely guaranteed by exegesis, and which offer us a *most trustworthy image* of the historical Jesus. We want to see what *really* happened' (p. 14; italics mine). This reminds me a little of Küng's promise to provide at last a picture of *the real Jesus* and the problems which are involved in such a promise.

Sobrino warns that a *selective* use of data from Jesus' history cannot hope to reproduce properly this history (pp. 83f.). But there is also the question of the *interpretation* of the data. How does Sobrino know, for instance, that at his baptism 'Jesus became aware of his mission and his sonship' (p. 96)? Jesus was certainly baptized, but we have no information about his self-awareness a week or, let us say, six months before that. Likewise how does Sobrino know that on the cross Jesus 'felt *completely* abandoned by the God, whose nearness he had felt and proclaimed' (p. 370; italics mine)? What hard evidence does Sobrino (and Moltmann whom he quotes) have for explaining the cry of abandonment (Mk 15, 34) to mean that Jesus experienced his death 'as *hellish* abandonment by the very God whose loving nearness he had proclaimed' (p. 218; italics mine)? Elsewhere Sobrino mitigates this interpretation of Mark 15, 34 by calling it 'a prayer of anguish' (p. 152) and a recital of Psalm 22 (p. 156). Which interpretation of the cry of abandonment is then to be preferred?

Put starkly and strongly, the key question eventually comes to this: Does Sobrino convincingly justify the starting point (and center) of his Christology? He modestly admits that he cannot find— and would not want to find—"some clear and indisputable Archimedean point for starting Christology" (p. 12). All the same, he sets out various reasons for his choice. Do these reasons work?

(a) First, Sobrino admits that 'according to the New Testament' the 'culmination' of Christology 'is reached in the resurrected Jesus'

(p. 259). Faith in Christ arose 'logically and chronologically with his resurrection' (p. 7). That would seem to imply that as 'faith in Christ seeking understanding', Christology itself should begin from the resurrection of the crucified Jesus. But Sobrino does not agree. He refers to 'the various Christologies' of the resurrection which 'separate the final stage of Jesus' life from his overall historical process' (p. 82). Some of these Christologies like Pannenberg's may tend to do that. But I do not believe Kasper makes that mistake, and I hope that my own forthcoming Christology (which centers on the paschal mystery) does not do so either. A valid resurrection Christology can (and should) respect Sobrino's insistence that Jesus' historical activity and the opposition it aroused led to the crucifixion and resurrection (pp. 201ff.). The paschal mystery was the climax and consequence of Jesus' life.

(b) Sobrino holds that 'the proper logical order of Christology is the *chronological* order' (p. 334; italics mine; see also p. xxii), and this means starting with the history of Jesus. Here I cannot help wondering whether there is some confusion between (i) the order of *the events themselves* (the incarnation, life, crucifixion, resurrection, sending of Holy Spirit and final coming of Christ), and (ii) the order of *faith's knowledge* and the consequent writing of those faith documents we call the New Testament. The chronological order of the events themselves would entail starting with the incarnation—something Sobrino does not want to do. But in terms of faith and the order of Christian knowledge of Jesus, one begins surely where faith arose 'logically and chronologically' (p. 7)—with the resurrection of the crucified Christ. As I noted in Chapter 1, Paul's letters witness to the way faith's appreciation of Jesus began with the paschal mystery; after that it moved backwards to the life, the birth and pre-existence of Christ.

(c) Third, Sobrino believes that starting with the concrete figure of the historical Jesus will avoid two extremes—'turning Christ into an *abstraction* on the one hand, or putting him to direct and immediate *ideological uses* on the other' (p. 10; italics mine).

Admittedly a resurrection Christology could lapse into abstraction, but only to the extent that it forgets that it is dealing with the personal resurrection of *this crucified Jesus.* St. Paul managed to maintain both sides of the paschal mystery and avoid lapsing into abstraction. This encourages me to think that a contemporary Pauline-style Christology can do the same.

Is a Christology which starts with the historical Jesus peculiarly insured against the 'danger of manipulating the Christ event' (p. 9)? I am afraid we can co-opt the historical Jesus almost as easily as we can the risen Christ. What stops us from organizing the story of Jesus 'in terms of some preconceived idea which we then find reflected in his history' (p. 83)? Sobrino himself recalls how Adolf von Harnack unwittingly manipulated the history of Jesus for ideological purposes (pp. 8, 61).

Nevertheless, Sobrino is correct in observing how the story of Jesus continues to challenge Christians. To forget that story weakens faith and real discipleship. To put matters positively, over and over again in the history of the Church reform movements have been inspired by that story. Sobrino cites the case of St. Ignatius Loyola, who 'viewed the concrete life of Jesus as the factor which could and should revitalize the life of the Christian' (p. 402).

To sum up. Although we should join Sobrino in insisting that the history of Jesus remains essential material for any adequate Christology (and any true Christian discipleship), nevertheless that is not the same as agreeing to construct 'a Christology of the historical Jesus' (p. 83). For the reasons indicated, the paschal mystery should be the starting point and center of Christology.

I hope that Sobrino's Christology has been fairly presented and evaluated. To do otherwise would seem monstrous treatment of someone who has written for a suffering people and out of a situation of hideous oppression and injustice. Hence I must protest against some points raised by reviews of his book. For instance, Henry Wansbrough may rightly take issue with the opposition Sobrino introduces between 'religion' and 'faith' (*The Tablet,* 22 July 1978, p. 702). But it is not true to say that Sobrino 'never defines what he means by religion'. He does so on pages 275f. Second, I share Wansbrough's dislike for the term 'points up', but it does not appear 'on nearly every page of this translation'. There are nine occurrences in 444 pages of text. Finally, it is not accurate simply to report Sobrino as having 'a good number of hard words to say about' dogma. In handling the early Christological definitions of the Church, Sobrino has a good number of good words to say about dogma and its essential value (pp. 311ff., 385ff.). I should add that Wansbrough calls the book under review 'a fresh and challenging Christology' which 'as a whole is most valuable'.

(3) To complete this chapter I plan to add some further material on *Jesus. An Experiment in Christology* (New York: Seabury, 1979), the first volume in Schillebeeckx's huge trilogy. Apropos of this English translation, it should be noted that even though it is offered as a version of the original Dutch text of 1974, in fact it also includes modifications found in later (Dutch) editions of this work. Schillebeeckx reacted in a thoroughly professional way to reviews and other evaluations by adding material to clarify, for example, his position on Christ's resurrection.

After briefly explaining why the book was written Schillebeeckx spends pages 43–558 establishing various conclusions from the New Testament (above all from the Synoptic Gospels) both about the history of Jesus and about the early Christian interpretations of him as the crucified-and-risen One. A brief account of Christological reflection in the post-New Testament period (pp. 559–71) leads to the final section, 'Who do we say he is?' (pp. 575–674). Even if the author calls this section only a prolegomenon to a Christology, it contains some helpful initial reflections on Jesus as divine person.

All in all, however, Schillebeeckx has little to say about Christological doctrines, Church tradition and, for that matter, the work of other theologians. His major concerns and contributions lie elsewhere: in his thoroughgoing attempt to reach *historically* based conclusions about Jesus of Nazareth.

Schillebeeckx shows a remarkable knowledge of current Scripture scholarship—European, British and North American. Yet sometimes his trust in certain contemporary exegetes leads him to rely far too much on what can at best be only tentative theories about matters like the nature of the Q community and the different stages in the formation of the Q tradition. In my opinion, he would have been better advised to follow widely accepted results coming from mainline exegesis.

Here, as with Mackey and Sobrino, I want to refer my com-

ments to some of the six themes I used in the opening chapters of this
book, taking them in this order: four (virginal conception), five (ministry) and three (resurrection).

Virginal Conception

As regards the virginal conception Schillebeeckx argues that the
tradition preserved by Matthew and Luke does not intend 'to impart
any empirically apprehensible truth or secret information about the
family history, but a truth of revelation' (p. 555). This tradition offers 'a theological reflection, not a supply of new informative data'
(p. 554). Here our author allows only for the alternative: *either* some
'informative data' which would constitute an 'empirically apprehensible truth', *or* 'a truth of revelation' which fuels 'theological reflection'. But must it be a matter of an either/or? Why cannot we have a
tradition which embodies *both* informative data *and* some truth of
revelation?

Incidentally, Schillbeeckx lists Raymond Brown among the exegetes whose work on the traditions concerning the virginal conception have made it clear that 'there is no question of "historical
information" here' (p. 554). Brown has never held this view. Rather
his conclusion is that we cannot scientifically trace the historical origin(s) and development of the traditions on which Matthew and
Luke draw at this point.

The Ministry

In centering everything on the Synoptic Gospels, the book deals
well with the parables, Jesus' attitudes towards the law, his dealings
with 'outcasts' and his role as *the* eschatological prophet. Schillebeeckx clearly states the real difference between the 'historical Jesus'
and the 'earthly Jesus': 'What can be reconstructed historically . . .
does not naturally coincide with the full reality of Jesus' (p. 68).
Any attempt to establish from the Synoptic or pre-Synoptic material
some uninterpreted, 'undogmatic' Jesus is rightly dismissed by
Schillebeeckx as an illusion (pp. 52f.). Moreover, it is 'impossible' to
take 'the most primitive picture of Jesus' as 'a norm or constant uni-

tive factor'. Such a 'first articulation' of Jesus or any other historical figure is not *ipso facto* 'the richest or most subtle one' (pp. 53f.). In his own portrayal of Jesus our author adopts that distinction without a difference (which the Bultmannians and some others have made an article of faith) between the psychology of Jesus and his self-understanding. Schillebeeckx rejects as 'hopeless' the 'enterprise of dissecting' the psychology of Jesus, but then argues that 'what he said (his message) and what he did (his mode of conduct) are enough to shed light on his self-understanding: his activities spring from his *extraordinarily pronounced consciousness* of a prophetic role' (p. 257; italics mine). When we speak of such a 'self-understanding' and characterize Jesus as 'no fanatic' (p. 301) and as 'a rational and purposeful individual' (p. 299) who at the end showed himself utterly certain that he was undergoing death 'as a final and extreme service to the cause of God as the cause of men' (p. 311), surely we are saying something about the psychology of Jesus even if we refuse to 'dissect' it? Of course, this much must be said for Schillebeeckx and the others. They force us to respect the *limited* nature of the data and not speculate indulgently about the psychological states of Jesus.

The Resurrection

Over against his own preference for the historical Jesus, Schillebeeckx contrasts the position of those who take the resurrection as their point of departure. Such a view is 'based on a prior conviction that salvation in Jesus is bound up *exclusively* with his resurrection' so that 'the Easter *kerygma* is the *sole* and *comprehensive* ground of salvation' (p. 73; italics mine). However, against Schillebeeckx it should be pointed out that many theologians who start from the resurrection of Jesus recognize the centrality of the paschal mystery *without* making it 'the sole and comprehensive ground of salvation'. For them the resurrection is pre-eminent *without* being exclusively so, and the Easter kerygma should *also* be 'informed by the recollection of events associated with the life and death of Jesus' (p. 73). Schillebeeckx has made it easier for himself to reject an approach through the resurrection by presenting only its more extreme exponents (N. Schmithals and G. Strecker).

On the resurrection Schillebeeckx's own position on the empty
tomb and the appearances should be challenged. First, he joins those
who detect a 'sacred tomb' tradition behind Mark 16, 1–8. There is
much to be said for this view, according to which early Christians
went on pilgrimage to the sepulchre of Jesus and at times celebrated
liturgies there. But once again our author sets up alternatives which
are unjustifiably narrow: 'The new problem is whether we have a tradition of an "empty tomb" or a tradition of a "holy tomb" ' (p. 703,
n. 32). But why not both: a tradition of a 'holy tomb' which was also
an 'empty tomb'? According to Schillebeeckx, 'John . . . makes it
very clear that an "empty tomb" if there were such a thing, could
never be proof of the resurrection (Jn. 20, 8–9), but at most a token
of an already existing faith in the resurrection' (p. 332). John, however, is far from making these three propositions 'very clear': (1) We
should doubt the empty tomb ('if there were such a thing'), (2) an
empty tomb could never be *proof* of the resurrection, and (3) such an
empty tomb could at most express a prior faith in the resurrection.
Proposition (2) looks correct, but propositions (1) and (3) should be
rejected. John's story affirms Mary Magdalene's discovery of the
empty tomb, a discovery which Peter and 'the other disciple' then
confirm. As for proposition (3), it seems clear enough that seeing the
empty tomb and the neatly separated shroud and napkin *led* the other disciple to Easter faith ('he saw and believed'). He is not represented as having 'an already existing faith in the resurrection' *before* his
visit to the tomb.

Schillebeeckx concludes his discussion of the holy sepulchre story in Mark 16, 1–8 thus: 'In the Jerusalem story this place is now
suddenly filled with a message from God: "He is alive! He has been
raised!" The tomb is filled by "the (gleaming) white of the young
man", which concentrates attention *completely* on itself and not on
whatever else may or may not be present in this tomb' (pp. 336f.;
italics mine). Here Schillebeeckx simply disregards the words 'He is
not here; see the place where they laid him' (Mark 16, 6). Even if our
author lets slip a remark about 'the emptiness' of the place which
truly captures much of its significance ('the empty space is the re-
verse side of the new plenitude: He has risen!' [p. 377]), several reasons prompt him to doubt or reject the empty tomb. To begin with,
he feels sure that 'an eschatological, bodily resurrection . . . has noth-

ing to do . . . with a corpse' (p. 704, n. 45). Then for 'modern people' an empty tomb can only prove 'largely disconcerting'. Structural analysis and semiotics will make it all meaningful for them by showing that Mark's story is (was?) simply unconcerned with the presence or absence of Jesus' corpse (pp. 336f.). Even more important for Schillebeeckx is his conviction that 'the resurrection kerygma was already present even before the traditions about the tomb and appearances had arisen. The Easter faith emerged independently of these two traditions' (pp. 333f.). How does Schillebeeckx think the disciples' Easter faith—or, as he puts it, their being converted through grace, and on Jesus' initiative, to Jesus as the Christ—came into existence?

Peter led the process of turning to Jesus as 'the living Lord' (p. 328). He and the other disciples received the grace of forgiveness (a 'concrete experience of forgiveness after Jesus' death'), discussed among themselves this renewed offer of salvation, experienced a deep conversion and reached the conclusion: 'Jesus must therefore be alive. . . . A dead man does not proffer forgiveness' (p. 391). *Then* the disciples went on to interpret and express this resurrection faith by speaking of appearances and the discovery of the empty tomb. Here Schillebeeckx's position must be fairly stated. He dissociates himself *completely* from the view that the resurrection is only 'a symbolic expression of the renewal of life for the disciples, albeit empowered by the inspiration they drew from the earthly Jesus' (pp. 644f.). It took the personal resurrection of Jesus himself to make possible the Easter experience of renewed life enjoyed by the disciples (pp. 644–47).

As regards our author's reconstruction of what happened after the crucifixion, I have one truly major puzzle. How could Peter, the other disciples or anyone else for that matter ever have a 'concrete experience of forgiveness' which does not *precisely as such* entail a personal encounter with the one who forgives them? Surely any concrete experience of forgiveness—and, incidentally, I can only wonder what a non-concrete experience of forgiveness would be like—takes place in immediate and *as such* conscious contact with the other person who offers forgiveness?

Further, there are a number of dubious arguments used to support Schillebeeckx's key affirmation that 'the resurrection was believed in before there was any question of appearances' (p. 354). In

the first place, he leaves me quite unconvinced when he interprets
the tradition about the witnesses in 1 Cor 15, 3–8 to mean that the
'apostles proclaim the crucified-and-risen One', and this mission is
subsequently legitimated by what 'has come to be called an "appearing of Jesus" ' (p. 350). Then very rapidly Schillebeeckx thinks he
can sweep aside (what he recognizes as) the common view that for
Paul 'the actual mandate for his apostolate' was the appearance of
Jesus to him (pp. 361f.). Third, our author has some fascinating comments to make about the three stories (Acts 9; 22; 26) of Paul's experience on the Damascus road. But methodologically it seems
unsound to use Luke's narratives to interpret *both* what Paul himself
says (in Galatians 1 and 1 Corinthians 15) about his conversion and
apostolic calling, *and* Peter's Easter experience which led him to re-
assemble the other disciples. Then Schillebeeckx remains silent about
Jesus' 'presenting himself alive' (Acts 1, 3) and being 'made manifest'
(Acts 10, 40) when he assures us that in Luke's understanding 'to be
a witness to the resurrection' is to witness 'to the resurrection as a
salvific event in God's plan of salvation, but not to testify that one
has met Jesus alive after his death and burial' (p. 356).

It would be tedious to go on listing the various weaknesses in
the arguments adduced. Let me conclude by pointing to what I take
to be the major flaw in our author's position. In an important sense it
is certainly true to say that the 'appearance *stories* and *accounts* of
the empty tomb assume the fact of the reassembled community and
its Christological *kerygma*' (p. 382; italics mine). Of course those
stories and accounts were shaped by Christians (through preaching
and other activities) during the thirties, forties and fifties before they
were adopted (and modified) by the Gospel writers. But that does *not*
mean that *as events* the appearances themselves and the discovery of
the empty tomb as such assumed a reassembled community already
believing in the resurrection and proclaiming its Christological
kerygma. In the book there seems to be an underlying confusion
between the order of (elaborated) narration and the prior order
of (historical) events.

This chapter has evaluated three attempts to approach Christology on the basis of what we can know about the life of Jesus—above
all, through the Synoptic Gospels. Mackey, Sobrino and Schillebeeckx all maintain that what we can establish about Jesus' history

offers a reasonable starting point and (partial) justification for the developed Christological doctrines which emerged in the fourth and fifth centuries. Mackey and (more successfully) Sobrino highlight the faith of the earthly Jesus, Schillebeeckx his special experience of God as 'Abba'. All three authors have produced works which yield a strong call to personal commitment.

Nevertheless, these theologians each exemplify the fact that a Christology (simply or largely) based on the historical Jesus will not finally work. Sobrino falters in his rejection of approaches through the resurrection of the crucified Christ. The treatments of the resurrection by Mackey and Schillebeeckx are even less convincing.

What emerges from this chapter could be summed up as follows. Any Christology should take into account the record of Jesus' ministry. But a Christology based more or less exclusively on the historical Jesus cannot hope to succeed. The next chapter will have more to say about Jesus and history.

5
The International
Theological Commission

Another way into contemporary discussions about the person of Jesus Christ (Christology) and his saving mission (soteriology) is provided by the latest document to come from the International Theological Commission: *Select Questions on Christology* (September 1, 1980; I will use the translation provided by the United States Catholic Conference). This Commission, whose members are appointed by the Pope to serve for five years, was established as an adjunct to the Congregation for the Doctrine of the Faith in 1969. Its purpose is to provide that Congregation and the Holy See with the consultative and advisory services of theologians, exegetes and liturgical experts representative of various schools of thought. Among those serving on the Commission when it produced *Select Questions on Christology* were such well-known theologians as Juan Alfaro, Hans Urs von Balthasar, Walter Burghardt, Yves Congar, Edouard Hamel, Karl Lehmann, Gustave Martelet, Cardinal Joseph Ratzinger, Jean-Marie Tillard and Jan Walgrave.

In its latest document the Commission clearly announced that it did 'not intend to expound and explicate a complete Christology' (p. 13). Nevertheless, it did indicate many current issues and hence serves as well as any other contemporary statement to inform us about the current state of question in Christology and soteriology.

Without pretending to offer anything like a complete commentary on the document, I want to single out and discuss some major themes to be found in *Select Questions on Christology.*

Jesus and History

Right from the outset the Commission recognizes that 'historical research concerning Jesus Christ is demanded by the Christian faith itself' (p. 1). This was always true, inasmuch as Christianity is an historical religion which from its beginning has recalled and lived by what the God of Abraham, Isaac and Jacob did and revealed in the particular life, death and resurrection of Jesus of Nazareth. Nevertheless, from the end of the eighteenth century Christology began to be deeply affected by the rise of scientific history and, in particular, by critical methods in biblical research. Debates about the earthly history of Jesus have often occupied center stage. Scientific history has emerged as Christology's most prominent dialogue partner in modern times.

Along with this special concern for historical issues, Christology—as we have seen—has undergone a certain proper *humanizing.* From the Middle Ages professional Catholic theology had tended to present Christ largely in terms of his divinity, and it was left to popular devotions to defend his genuinely human existence and experience. Thus the Christmas crib, the stations of the cross and the devotion to the Sacred Heart witnessed to the ordinary faithful's instinctive attachment to the authentic humanity of Jesus. Since the Second Vatican Council the best scholars—without going to the extreme of attempting to produce a Christology simply and solely on the basis of the historical life of Jesus—have incorporated 'a return to the earthly Jesus'. This the Theological Commission considers not only 'beneficial' but also 'indispensable today in the field of dogmatic theology'. Our document frankly admits past deficiencies in this matter: 'The untold riches of Jesus' humanity need to be brought to light more effectively than was done by the Christologies of the past' (p. 4).

How far can historical scholarship take us in reconstructing the ministry and message of the earthly Jesus? The Commission first recalls the *intention* of our basic sources, the Gospels. They offer an amalgam of believing witness and historical reminiscence with the aim of eliciting or at least developing the faith of their readers. They cannot be treated as if they were ordinary, disinterested historical sources from ancient times. Further, the Gospels do not provide sufficient data to write a biography 'in the modern sense of this word'. Nevertheless, 'we should not draw from this fact excessively pessimistic conclusions as to the possibility of coming to know the historical life of Jesus' (p. 2).

Essentially the Commission is making a double point here. On the one hand, we would not be justified in renewing the nineteenth century attempts to write a life of Jesus. But, on the other hand, historical research can use the Gospels to establish a good deal about the activity, message, claim and impact of Jesus during the last period of his life. Scholarly principles can vindicate the following conclusions. Jesus came from Nazareth, was baptized by John, and began a wandering ministry in which he proclaimed that 'the kingdom of God' was at hand, associated with sinners and outcasts, called disciples to follow him, worked miracles and taught some memorable parables. His violation of certain sabbath laws, cleansing of the temple and other 'offences' aroused the antagonism of some influential Jewish leaders. In Jerusalem (where he had come for the Passover celebration) he was arrested, interrogated by members of the Sanhedrin, tried by Roman authorities, and then executed as a messianic pretender on a cross which bore an inscription giving the charge against him as 'King of the Jews'. This is not anything like a complete list of items about the earthly Jesus which scientific methods can validate. But it should indicate the kind of material the Theological Commission has in mind when it notes how scholarly research can verify "the historicity of certain facts relative to the historical existence of Jesus" (p. 2).

Ever so much more could be said about the necessity and the limits of historical inquiry. Let me content myself with singling out two items from *Select Questions on Christology*.

In the first place, the document insists on the unity between the earthly Jesus and the glorified Christ. Because of his 'substantive and radical unity', any Christological inquiry which limited itself to the

Jesus of history 'would be incompatible with the essence and structure of the New Testament' (p. 2).

The Commission rightly sees how this 'original and primitive synthesis of the earthly Jesus with the risen Christ' implies an ecclesial setting for anyone's theology at this point: 'We cannot secure a *full* knowledge of Jesus unless we take into account the living faith of the Christian community' (pp. 2f.; italics mine). Our document goes on to state this even more strongly:

> The Church continues to be the place where the *true* knowledge of the person and work of Jesus Christ is to be found. Apart from the assistance provided by the mediation of ecclesial faith, the knowledge of Jesus Christ is *no more possible* today than in New Testament times (p. 4; italics mine).

At the same time, the Commission acknowledge the primacy of Christology over ecclesiology, the priority of Jesus Christ over his Church. Even though we will fully and truly know him only in 'the ecclesial context', 'Our Lord always preserves vis-à-vis the Church the priority of his position and his primacy' (p. 4).

So much then for the unity between the Jesus of history and the glorified Christ whom the Christian community confessed and continues to confess in faith. My second point is a tiny doubt about what our document envisages when it speaks of 'mere historical information', 'a purely historical image of Jesus', 'a purely historical kind of research', 'pure history' and 'a mere historical evocation' (pp. 2f.). Is the document forgetting that historians deal with 'the remembered *and interpreted* past' and weave their own evaluations into the work of recovering data from the past? My doubts here are fed by the Commission's reference to "the modern notion of history . . . according to which history is the bare and objective presentation of a reality now past' (p. 3). This 'modern notion of history' in fact sounds all too like the view of Leopold von Ranke and other *nineteenth* century scholars who fondly imagined that they could describe with 'scientific', objective neutrality what had actually happened. More recently this positivist understanding of history has been widely abandoned, and at least some proper role of *subjective* interpretation and appropriation has generally been acknowledged. Perhaps Hans Küng and Willi Marxsen in their weaker moments exemplify 'the modern notion of history' which the Commission speaks of and objects to. But it is hard to think of many contemporary writers on Christology who lapse back into such an approach.

Perhaps I am being unduly sensitive on this issue. But when dealing with the earthly Jesus (and, for that matter, other persons and events in past history), I certainly want to fight shy of language which could suggest anything like a separation between the bare facts, on the one hand, and someone's vision or interpretation of these facts, on the other. Right from the level of sense experience a totally uninterpreted grasp of anyone or anything is impossible. In their very first contacts with Jesus the earliest disciples were already interpreting him. The Church traditions and then the Gospel writers (rightly and inevitably) carried on this process of interpretation. There never was 'mere' historical information about Jesus, in the sense of some set of objective, uninterpreted facts about him. In the last chapter we saw how Schillebeeckx rightly insists on this point.

Nicaea, Chalcedon and Beyond

The Commission recalls the work of the earthly Church councils which aimed to state the double reality of Christ's being 'true God and true man', so that one aspect would not prevail at the expense of the other. Our document correctly maintains that the doctrine of Christ's divinity was developed from the biblical revelation and, so far from being a product of Greek philosophy, was an affront to major philosophical schools. With their strong sense of divine transcendence the Platonists regarded a divine incarnation as 'unthinkable' (p. 5; see p. 7). The Stoics with their doctrine of divine immanence could accept the hypostatic union, but not that distinction between Christ's two natures which was entailed by the divine transcendence (pp. 5, 6f.).

There are several points recalled by the Commission when it endorses the Christological teachings of the early councils. It notes, for example, the 'in-depth interaction between lived experience and the process whereby theological clarification was achieved' (p. 5). Theological reflection and doctrines sprang from the immediacy of a personal relationship with the Son of God and were intended in their turn to clarify and promote the faith which constituted that relationship. Both then and now, teachings *about* Christ come from a living experience *of* him and should feed back into that experience.

Select Questions on Christology also recognizes not only that the Chalcedonian definition about the two natures in one person did 'not pretend to offer an exhaustive answer' to the question of the union of humanity and divinity in Christ (p. 7), but also that the Council's formula needs to be enriched 'through more soteriological perspectives' (p. 11). Explicitly as such the definition gave only a passing nod to human redemption (when it spoke of Jesus Christ as being 'begotten for us men and for our salvation'). To put matters in an extreme form: everything that Chalcedon affirmed could still be valid if Jesus had been miraculously snatched away from this world and never died on Calvary to save us. At best, his death is only hinted at in phrases like 'truly man' and 'like us in all respects, apart from sin'. Chalcedon's formula passes over in silence the resurrection which took place 'for our justification' (Rom 4, 25). The Theological Commission helpfully observes that the Chalcedonian Christology must be supplemented by an adequate soteriology. I will return to this issue shortly. It corresponds, of course, to the sixth theme discussed in the opening chapters of this book.

A final point which concerns Chalcedon's terminology: *Select Questions on Christology* makes the astonishing claim that 'terms such as "nature" and "person" which the Fathers of the Council use undoubtedly retain the same meaning in today's parlance'. Yet at once the Commission goes on to summarize what is very often denoted today by 'human nature' and 'person' (p. 9). Perhaps I am missing something here. But the meaning shifts noted in the second half of the paragraph undercut the claim that 'nature' and 'person' retain 'the same meaning in today's parlance'. Doubtless there is a healthy family resemblance between the fifth century's use and meaning for these terms and what we find today, but hardly an identity. Back in Chapter 1, I drew attention to the development from the ancient to the modern concepts of 'person'.

Soteriology

One of the best passages in our document is that which lists the severe difficulties which many people experience in understanding what salvation through Christ is about. Let me quote it in full.

> Today many . . . recoil from any notion of salvation which would imply a heteronomy in the project of life. They take exception to what they regard as the purely individualistic character of Christian salvation. The promise of blessedness to come seems to them a utopia which distracts people away from their genuine obligations which, in their view, are all confined to this world. They want to know what it is that mankind had to be redeemed from, and to whom the price of salvation had to be paid. They grow indignant at the idea that God could have exacted the blood of an innocent person, a notion in which they detect a streak of sadism. They argue against what is known as 'vicarious satisfaction' (that is, through a mediator) by saying that this mode of satisfaction is ethically impossible. If it is true that every conscience is autonomous, they argue, no conscience can be freed by another. Finally, some of our contemporaries lament the fact that they cannot find in the life of the Church and of the faithful the lived expression of the mystery of liberation which is proclaimed (pp. 9f.; translation corrected).

Given the scope of its document, the Theological Commission could not (and could not be expected to) respond in detail to all of these difficulties. But it was good to see a frank and fair account of the genuine problems which any treatment of soteriology must confront.

What does our document have to say about soteriology? It opens its section on 'Christology and Soteriology' with the clear affirmation that 'the person of Jesus Christ cannot be separated from the deed of redemption. The benefits of salvation are inseparable from the divinity of Jesus Christ'. No one could quarrel with the mild verdict on the past: 'Some theological speculations have failed to adequately preserve this intimate connection between Christology and soteriology' (p. 12). Various Protestant theologians from Philipp Melanchthon (1497–1560) to Rudolf Bultmann (1884–1976) could be so preoccupied with what Christ did and does 'for us' that they practically reduced Christology to soteriology. On the Catholic side the opposite situation often prevailed. Christology took pride of place and soteriology got treated subsequently—sometimes very briefly.

The Theological Commission develops its own brief sketch of soteriology on the basis of the human intentions of Jesus when faced with his passion and death. Our document tackles the issue on two levels: that of principle and that of the ascertainable facts. In principle, *if* Jesus 'lost hope in his own mission' and saw his passion simply as 'a failure and a shipwreck',

> ... his death could not be construed then, and cannot be construed now, as the definitive act in the economy of salvation. A death undergone in a purely passive manner could not be a 'Christological' saving event. It must be the consequence, the willed consequence, of the obedience and love of Jesus making a gift of himself. It must be taken up in a complex act, at once active and passive (p. 13).

At the level of the ascertainable facts, the Commission points to items in the Gospel record which indicated how Jesus interpreted his coming death. Our document speaks of Jesus' 'fundamental attitude' of 'existence-for-others' which was given 'more vitality and concreteness' as questions emerged for him and events unfolded. Among the questions which came to confront him were these:

> Would the Father want to establish his reign, if Jesus should meet with failure, with death, nay, with the cruel death of martyrdom? Would the Father, in the end, ensure the saving efficacy of what Jesus would have suffered by 'dying for others'?

Jesus 'gathered affirmative answers to these questions' and hence went to death confidently reasserting at the Last Supper 'the promise and presence of the eschatological salvation' (p. 14).

To put matters bluntly, this approach—very correctly, I believe—acknowledges a certain shift of perspective on the part of the earthly Jesus. Historically his fundamental attitude of self-giving led him *from* an awareness that through his preaching, actions and personal presence he was establishing God's final salvation *to* a subsequent acceptance of his victim-role. The Jesus who began by proclaiming the eschatological reign of God ended by obediently agreeing to be the victim whose death and vindication would bring salvation. At least on pp. 13–15 (section IV B) our document seems to allow for some shift or at least clarification in Jesus' (human) mind about the specific shape of his vocation and destiny. This section which betrays the influence of Heinz Schurmann is followed by a section (pp. 15–19, IV C) in which I cannot fail to detect the hand of Hans Urs von Balthasar and which contains several themes that invite a little scrutiny.

To begin with, this section maintains that 'Jesus knows that he is to die for all, for our sins; in this perspective, he lives out his *entire* earthly life' (pp. 16f.; italics mine). At the very least this statement stands in a certain tension with what we have just seen.

Second, although I welcomed the document's readiness to defend one of the basic models for redemption, vicarious expiation—which is better called representative expiation—I was sorry to see it expounded as if it amounted to expiatory *substitution*. Space does not permit me to discuss matters as extensively as I did in *The Calvary Christ* (pp. 92–114). Here let me pick out only two points in the treatment of this interpretation of redemption as expiatory substitution.

The earthly Jesus is credited with 'the will to take on himself as a proxy the sufferings (cf. Gal 3, 13) and the sin of the human kind (cf. Jn 1, 29; 2 Cor 5, 21)' (p. 16). There are several questionable items here. The two texts from St. Paul indicate nothing about the intentions of the earthly Jesus. It is a bold person indeed who would use the statement of John's Gospel ('Behold, the Lamb of God, who takes away the sin of the world') to support a claim about the *historical* intentions of the *earthly* Jesus. Further, the 'for us' of Galatians 3, 13 points not to a proxy suffering 'in our place' but to a representative suffering for our sake and to our advantage. John 1, 29 speaks of Christ not as assuming or as 'taking *on*' the sin of the world but as taking it *away*. Paul's dense statement in 2 Corinthians 5, 21 ('For our sake he [God] made him [Christ] to be sin who knew no sin.') demands unpacking, and we can do that in any of the following ways: 'God made the innocent Christ a sin-offering for us'; 'God sent the sinless Christ into a sinful world'; 'God submitted the innocent Christ to the regime of the law which was the regime of sin'. The apostle is not maintaining something that in any case seems impossible—that the innocent Christ literally 'took on' the sin of the human kind. A guiltless person can suffer *from* the sins of others, and can suffer *for* others, but cannot literally carry the moral guilt *of* others.

Another point which comes across as thoroughly questionable is the document's claim that

> . . . no matter how great be the sinner's estrangement from God, it is not as deep as the sense of distance which the Son experiences vis-à-vis the Father in the kenotic emptying of himself (Phil 2, 7) and in the anguish of 'abandonment' (Mt 27, 46) (p. 18).

This is a latter-day example of a cherished theme of some Christian rhetoric. But does the New Testament support it? In Philippians Paul is not appealing to early Christian hymnic language to speak of a deeply experienced 'sense of distance'. The cry of abandonment in Matthew's account of the passion is a quotation from a psalm which does not allow us to compare Jesus' interior state on the cross with the sinner's feeling of estrangement from God.

To conclude: The Theological Commission's document on Christology, if here and there needing some tightening, covers many of the important current issues. Besides themes which have already been mentioned, the document also recalls the pneumatological and cosmic dimensions of Christology (pp. 19–22). It refers to two other extremely significant questions: (a) Christ's consciousness and knowledge, and (b) ways of expressing 'the absolute and universal value of the redemption effected by Christ for all and once for all' (p. 11). Echoing the Second Vatican Council's *Constitution on the Church in the Modern World* (n. 58), the Commission acknowledges 'the originality and value of various cultures' which implies the need to set forth the mystery of Christ through the 'particular riches and charisms' of all cultures (p. 12).

Personally I would have liked to have seen more detailed treatment of two themes: (a) Christ and non-Christians, and (b) the relationship between Christ's roles in creation and redemption. Then nothing was really said in the document about the genesis and nature of belief in Christ as *risen* from the dead. Of course, it might be argued that current issues on Christ's resurrection belong more to exegetes than to theologians—as work for the Biblical Commission rather than for the Theological Commission.

All in all, as a kind of official position paper *Select Questions on Christology* serves very well to direct Catholic and Christian reflection in that field. In a further document scheduled for publication around the end of 1982 the Theological Commission will apparently deal with the following themes: the revelation of the Trinity through Jesus Christ, his pre-existence, Christocentrism and Theocentrism, Christology and anthropology, and the consciousness of the earthly Jesus. That second document should also provide useful guidelines for work on Christological issues.

6
Commitment to Jesus

This book has tossed around the names of big-league exegetes and theologians: Brown, Kasper, Küng, Moltmann, Pannenberg, Schillebeeckx, Schoonenberg, Schürmann, Vawter and others. But the scholars cannot be allowed to have it all their own way when we examine the recent thinking about Jesus.

A book written with the verve and vigour of Muggeridge's *Jesus* can tempt us to feel that technical theology and critical exegesis at times let us down. This popular writer recaptures something which scholars (not, however, Mackey and Sobrino) may at times obscure: that religious dimension of Jesus' story which demands our commitment.

Historical Scholarship

It takes, of course, no great effort to rustle up sweeping criticisms against the methods of a Muggeridge. He uses John's gospel as if it were a reliable historical source, indulges wild anachronisms, and largely ignores two centuries of biblical scholarship which have laid bare the processes behind the formation of the New Testament texts. Despite (or because of?) his being somewhat fundamentalist, however, Muggeridge discerns and describes a person fit to be the object of our faith. His Jesus is genuinely 'believable'.

But where do the so-called 'strictly historical' techniques take us? They may entail analysing texts, dismantling beliefs and carrying on minute debates in such a way that the Jesus of the gospels suffers the death of a thousand comments and details. It often seems futile looking for Jesus and his message in the official journals of New Testament studies. In the mid-1960s I trotted off one summer and attended an international scripture conference at an ancient university. The vice-chancellor, a lawyer by profession, had been asked to welcome the overseas visitors and open proceedings. A conscientious person, he prepared himself for the occasion by reading several commentaries on the gospels. He became baffled by the scholarly passion for dismembering the New Testament texts and preventing them from speaking for themselves. He mentioned this. Then slightly outraged and greatly puzzled he added: 'But these are good books! There's no need to treat them like that!' Muggeridge is not slow to hold up his hand in horror at 'the deserts and jungles of Biblical criticism'.[58] He derides the scholarship which has produced rows of new translations: 'Future historians . . . are likely to conclude that the more we knew about Jesus the less we knew him, and the more precisely his words were translated the less we understood or heeded them.'[59]

All of this borders dangerously on an irrational plea for the heart rather than the head, a preference for the 'simple' faith of the French peasant over the complexities of the German professor. Nevertheless, set Muggeridge's *Jesus* alongside Vawter's *This Man Jesus* and the contrast is startling. Vawter's book is technically correct and shows up the fundamentalist mistakes of the brilliant amateur, Muggeridge. The blurb on the cover claims that 'this book . . . offers all believers help in their desire to be in authentic contact with the living Christ and embrace his message in the light in which it was first proclaimed'. I wonder how many have accepted the offered help. Vawter's book has not proved nearly as successful as Muggeridge's in bringing believers—or for that matter non-believers—into authentic contact with the living Christ. Why is such New Testament scholarship failing? Or *pace* the blurb, does *This Man Jesus* properly remain at one remove from religious commitment and need to be 'applied' pastorally before it directly affects the life of faith?

Vawter himself remarks: 'The route of this historical method is admittedly not an easy one, and not everyone will always agree exactly where it leads.'[60] It is in fact high time to blow the whistle on the folly which can seem to turn this method into a latter-day idol.

Some authors risk alleging that their use of historical techniques establishes contact with Jesus in a uniquely privileged way. Küng, for instance, contrasts 'the traditional' Jesus with 'the original' Jesus, compares the work of the critical scholar with that of an art expert, and concludes that the expert may uncover an original masterpiece which later hands have unwittingly painted over. Likewise 'it could come to light what the Church and theology have made out of Jesus and done with him—liturgically, dogmatically, politically, juridically and pedagogically'.[61]

Küng betrays here the enthusiasm for a brand of historical exegesis that so often mars as well as makes some recent Roman Catholic theology. To begin with, do we find Jesus through studying history rather than through work for the needy, common worship and personal prayer? Can exegesis assure us of some strikingly privileged contact with Jesus, denied to St. Francis of Assisi, St. Teresa of Avila and others unfortunate enough to live before the historical-critical method came along to uncover God's masterpiece? Secondly, Küng at this point lays claim to a fresh objectivity over against all that 'the Church and theology have made out of Jesus and done with him'. But what does the theologian Küng make out of Jesus and do with him? Should any theologian pretend to occupy a 'wiser-than-thou' position that puts him above and beyond the Church and other theologians?

Küng, however, goes on to allow that faith in Jesus does not depend upon the historical method.[62] At the end of the day he may in fact be highlighting only two functions of this method. First, it has the apologetic role of answering those who challenge the amount of public information available about Jesus. Second, it tracks down events which generated the New Testament texts. This grappling with the visible order of things can only serve to present the humanity of Jesus in a clearer light.

Elsewhere, Küng helpfully remarks that truth should not be reduced to historical truth:

> In given circumstances poetry can catch the secret of nature and of man better than some ever so exact description or photograph. . . . Truth is not identical with facticity, and in particular not identical with historical truth. . . . Poetry,

> parable and legend ... can communicate more relevant
> truth than an historical report.[63]

He then introduces a remarkably useful comparison between (a) the
gospels as dramatic representations of history and (b) historical plays
of Shakespeare like *Henry V.*[64] This comparison deserves development.

Before going to Stratford-upon-Avon, we might wonder how
freely Shakespeare has used his sources. We could decide to satisfy
our historical demon by investigating the actual story of Henry V.
We could settle for ourselves a hard core of facts. But then it would
be absurd to sit through a performance, noting down carefully every
point where the playwright has modified the record for his artistic
purposes. Critical history can likewise assure us about the basic
structure of Jesus' story. Brown, Kasper, Küng, Vawter and many
others endorse a common consensus which takes Matthew, Mark
and Luke to be substantially reliable in reporting what Jesus said and
did. Having pacified our historical itch, we can then take up a gospel
as a dramatic whole. It frames the story of Jesus and invites our in-
volvement in a way in which, of course, *Henry V* does not. The gospel narratives will come alive for us, if we allow ourselves to come
alive in the face of the texts. It may seem 'safer' to stick to a quest for
historical details. But that way we will not truly find anything out—
neither about Jesus nor about ourselves.

In brief, let the methods of critical history have their role, a sub-
ordinate rather than a dominant one. Sheer historical research can in
fact turn out to be a way of avoiding the real drama and the essential
issue raised by the gospels: Am I willing to put my whole life—with
all its fears and hopes—into the crucified hands of Jesus? Any biblical research that finally prevents this challenge from being heard is
both playing false to the nature of the gospels and substituting scholarly idols for the questions: 'What do you seek? Do you love me?' (Jn
1, 38; 21, 15).

Imagination and Commitment

Muggeridge's *Jesus* reminds us sharply that we are not saved by
historical scholarship alone. A book that can be technically faulted

by professional exegetes turns out to be religiously compelling. The reproductions of masterpieces which accompany the text suggest that sometimes we may approach Jesus more effectively through the imagination of artists rather than through the intellect of theologians. Muggeridge overstates his case to make this point: 'Only mystics, clowns and artists, in my experience, speak the truth, which, as Blake was always insisting, is perceptible to the imagination rather than the mind.'[65] Our knowledge of Jesus Christ is far too serious a business to be left to theologians and exegetes alone. From the Middle Ages these professionals have monotonously neglected art and the imagination as guides to religious truth. I find myself in complete agreement with those who wish to reinstate the 'mystics, clowns and artists' alongside the scholars. The imaginable is the believable. To modify Wittgenstein: What we cannot imagine, we must confine to silence and non-belief.

Finally, Muggeridge rests his case on the mutual dependence of commitment and knowledge. St. Augustine's 'Give me a lover and he will understand' applies here. A genuine moral sensibility and a true religious concern make it possible to know and understand Jesus. After all the criticisms are in, only the mean-minded can overlook the deep attachment to Jesus which lights up the pages of *On Being a Christian*. The enormous success of Küng's book derives at least partly from this affectionate commitment to Jesus and his cause. The Swiss theologian published *Christ sein* on the twentieth anniversary of his priestly ordination. 'This book', he insisted at the press conference, 'was not written because the author considers himself a good Christian, but because he thinks that being a Christian is a particularly good thing.' Muggeridge goes further than Küng in admitting his personal sinfulness. It makes him unworthy of the Lord. Yet this gives him an ultimate claim on the one who 'came not to call the righteous, but sinners' (Mk 2, 17). Does Muggeridge's *Jesus* verify at the level of popular writing the need for that multi-layered conversion which Bernard Lonergan has championed? Should we adapt Augustine and exclaim, 'Give me a repentant and prayerful theologian and he or she will understand Jesus'?

At the end of the day, it may be nothing less than the praise of forgiven sinners which will find the right language to use of Jesus Christ, the one who died that we might live.

7
Epilogue

To keep this work down to manageable proportions, I plan to end by noting some further matters for discussion and by concisely listing some other recent studies in the area of Christology.

Further Matters

(1) Apart from pp. 50–52, this book fails to deal with *Christ and Non-Christians*. In my *Fundamental Theology* (Ramsey, N.J.: Paulist, 1981) I dedicate a chapter to this vital question in what can be called the 'wider ecumenism'. In the light of our faith in Christ, what should we say about the ways in which revelation and salvation reach non-Christians?

Here let me direct the reader's attention to the following works:

R. Panikkar, *The Intrareligious Dialogue* (New York: Paulist, 1978); *Myth, Faith and Hermeneutics* (New York: Paulist, 1979); *The Unknown Christ of Hinduism* (Maryknoll, N.Y.: rev. ed., Orbis, 1981).

K. Rahner, *Foundations of Christian Faith* (New York: Seabury, 1978), pp. 138–75.

L. Richard, *What Are They Saying About Christ and World Religions?* (Ramsey, N.J.: Paulist, 1981).

One can also find much relevant material in Rahner's *Theological Investigations* (1961—), especially Vols. 5, 6, 9, 10, 12, 14, 16 and 17. See also the essay by P. Rossana, 'Theology and Religions:

A Contemporary Problem', in *Problems and Perspectives of Fundamental Theology* ed. R. Latourelle & G. O'Collins (Ramsey, N.J.: Paulist, 1982), pp. 292–308.

(2) Two other, important items which are both connected with the saving work of Jesus also merit serious discussion: *his blood* and the *Shroud of Turin*. When we remember how the New Testament repeatedly associated 'the blood of the cross' (Col 1, 20) with our redemption, the silence of contemporary theology about Jesus' blood can seem extraordinary. In the face of the enormous popular interest, it is also remarkable that current Christology has continued to ignore the Shroud. On these two points see my articles in *The Way:* 'The Shroud of Turin', 20 (1980), pp. 140–47; 'Our Peace and Reconciliation', 22 (1982), pp. 112–21.

(3) Talking of omissions, I should observe how this book has passed over recent writings on *'Spirit' Christology*. P. Rosato's 'Spirit Christology: Ambiguity and Promise', *Theological Studies* 38 (1977), pp. 423–49, remains a very helpful starting point. J. O'Donnell's 'Jesus and the Spirit' is scheduled to appear under 'Theological Trends' in *The Way* for October 1982 or January 1983.

(4) The current interest in spirituality has properly recalled a neglected *source* for Christology: *the writings of great mystics and other classics of Christian living*. W.M. Thompson draws on such works in his *Jesus, Lord and Savior* (New York: Paulist: 1980). See also G.H. Tavard's 'The Christology of the Mystics', *Theological Studies* 42 (1981), pp. 561–79. An adequate view of tradition requires Christology to go beyond the New Testament, the official teachings of the Church and technical theology to draw data also from the liturgy, lives of saints, spiritual writings and other records of faithful contacts with the risen Lord in the total life of the Church.

(5) Back in Chapter 1, I touched on the difficulties faced by any Christologies which take the incarnation (rather than the resurrection of Christ) as their starting point. *The Myth of God Incarnate*, ed. J. Hick (Philadelphia: Westminster, 1977) ran into just those difficulties, even if its overall thrust made the book a negative (rather than a positive) Christology. Many critics assailed the work for its inconsistent use of the key term 'myth' and/or for not really reckoning with the fact that in the popular sense of that term, the title implied a negative answer to Christian belief in Jesus Christ as divine. But often

the criticism missed the key mistake: that joint study began at the wrong place (the incarnation rather than the resurrection) in posing the question of identifying Jesus as eternal Son of God.

Then some of the contributors to *The Myth of God Incarnate* seemed to presuppose that *merely* historical inquiry could in principle determine whether or not Jesus actually was the divine Son of God. They appeared to expect that such an inquiry, by providing direct evidence from the New Testament and other documents of past history, could simply decide the issue. This was to ask far too much from such historical evidence and to forget—among other things— the role of present experience in affirming the resurrection of Jesus, the incarnation and other Christological mysteries.

Further Literature

(1) International *scripture scholarship* continues to enrich contemporary Christology. From Germany have come such splendid studies by Martin Hengel as *The Son of God* (Philadelphia: Fortress, 1976) and *The Atonement* (Philadelphia: Fortress, 1981). The veteran Cambridge scholar C.F.D. Moule received the Collins book award for *The Origin of Christology* (New York & Cambridge: CUP, 1977). After his fine *Jesus and the Spirit* (London: SCM, 1975), James Dunn of Nottingham University has put out *Christology in the Making* (Philadelphia: Westminster, 1980).

North America, among other notable studies, has produced Ben Meyer's *The Aims of Jesus* (London: SCM, 1979) and Raymond Brown's *The Birth of the Messiah* (Garden City, N.Y.: Doubleday, 1977). Apart from some dubious 'conservative' reflections on Matthew 16, 17–19, Meyer builds on Joachim Jeremias and other earlier writers to offer one of the best accounts of Jesus' ministry. In *Gregorianum* 59 (1978), p. 757, I greeted *The Birth of the Messiah* as a 'monumental achievement'. Regrettably the Italian translation of this work on the infancy narratives (of Matthew and Luke) was the object of an inaccurate and almost grotesque review in *Osservatore Romano* for 18 February 1982. Among the numerous recent publications from the United States one should not miss Joseph Fitzmyer's 'Jesus the Lord', *Chicago Studies* 17 (1978), pp. 75–104 and his *To Advance the Gospel* (New York: Crossroad, 1981).

(2) Among *general introductions to Christology*, Dermot Lane's *The Reality of Jesus* (New York: Paulist, 1977) has proved its value, even if it has little to say about Christ's saving work. John O'Grady's *Models of Jesus* (Garden City, N.Y.: Doubleday, 1981) is useful, if a little inaccurate in the sections dealing with the virginal conception and the knowledge of the earthly Jesus. In *Catholicism* (Minneapolis: Winston, 1980) I, pp. 367–563, Richard McBrien gives a clear and solid introduction to Christology.

(3) The following *survey articles* should be noted:

T.E. Clarke, 'Current Christologies', *Worship* 53 (1979), pp. 438–48.

B. Cooke, 'Horizons on Christology in the Seventies', *Horizons* 6 (1979), pp. 193–217.

A. Dulles, 'Contemporary Approaches to Christology', *Living Light* 13 (1976), pp. 119–44.

J.P. Galvin, 'The Resurrection of Jesus in Catholic Systematics', *Heythrop Journal* 20 (1979), pp. 123–45; 'Jesus' Approach to Death', *Theological Studies* 41 (1980), pp. 713–44.

B. McDermott, 'Roman Catholic Christology: Two Recurring Themes', *Theological Studies* 41 (1980), pp. 339–67.

B. Mondin, 'New Trends in Christology', *Biblical Theological Bulletin* 4 (1974), pp. 33–74.

J.P. Schineller, 'Christ and Church: A Spectrum of Views', *Theological Studies* 37 (1976), pp. 545–66.

B. Sesboüé, 'Histoire et foi en christologie', *Nouvelle Revue Theologique* 101 (1979), pp. 3–23; 'Bulletin de théologie dogmatique. Christologie. Hans Küng et Edward Schillebeeckx', *Recherches de Science Religieuse* 67 (1979), pp. 567–97; 'Le procès contemporain de Chalcédoine', *ibid.* 65 (1977), pp. 45–79.

(4) Other books which readers could find rewarding in the area of Christology are:

M. Cook, *The Jesus of Faith* (Ramsey, N.J.: Paulist, 1981).

D. Tracy, *The Analogical Imagination* (New York: Crossroad, 1981), pp. 233–338.

F.J. van Beeck, *Christ Proclaimed: Christology as Rhetoric* (New York: Paulist, 1979).

Even at the end of this epilogue I am aware of some important documents, authors and themes in current Christology which have been omitted or barely mentioned. But I did not want to make the mistake of putting everything and everyone in. To list all questions, flood the reader with names, and then account for influences—both direct and indirect—of texts and theologians on one another could only create boredom and confusion. If what has been said sheds light on some major shifts that have taken place in Christology during the last twenty-five years, I will be satisfied.

Appendix:
The Imagination of Jesus

For some people Christmas can act as an irritating reminder that we know so little about the life of Jesus—except for some crowded months at the end. Once his ministry begins, we see him delivering his unique message, healing the sick, pardoning sinners and—as the opposition gathers with stunning speed—quickly becoming a man on the run. Action fills that last year or two. But before then Jesus lives through three decades about which we know next to nothing. We can be haunted by our incredibly slight information about his birth, childhood, youth and early manhood.

Some Christians coped with their bewilderment by giving their fantasies free rein and inventing answers to all the questions we or others might care to ask. The so-called apocryphal gospels did their best to fill in the details about all those blanks in Jesus' life.

When the Holy Family arrived in Egypt, one account informs us that the temple idols crashed in pieces before the baby Jesus and that Pharaoh himself recognized him as truly God. The apocryphal gospels chatter on also about the silent years in Nazareth. Some of these stories may seem mere pious imaginings, but others can be downright nasty. One story portrays Jesus walking through a village when a child runs into him. Jesus curses him and the child dies on the spot. The people of the village complain to Joseph, telling him to leave at once as their children are in danger. When Joseph passes on the complaint to Jesus, the villagers who complained are struck

blind. Joseph sees what has happened, seizes Jesus' ear and gives it a
good tug. The last point in the story can seem amusing. But the
whole narrative exudes a taste for spiteful and murderous magic.
Here, as elsewhere, we can appreciate that the Christian Church did
well to refuse to accept such apocryphal gospels into the canon of the
New Testament.

But are we simply left then to put up with our very limited
knowledge about so much of Jesus' life? Not altogether. Some conclusions can be legitimately drawn from the first three gospels. There
his preaching offers some clues as to *the way in which his imagination
formed during the years in Nazareth.* The language and imagery used
by Jesus hints at the way he perceived the world.

Four Presuppositions

Before developing this argument and exploring the imagery of
Jesus, I should clarify some presuppositions.

(1) I am not holding that *all* the language which Matthew,
Mark and Luke attribute to Jesus necessarily goes back to the actual
ministry. Some of that language derives from the gospel writers
themselves, from the early Church traditions or from the risen Christ
himself.

(2) I am not claiming that the gospel writers ever give us an exact transcript of the words Jesus used. But I agree with many scholars that Matthew, Mark and Luke present *a substantially accurate
version* of what Jesus said. In what follows I wish to refer only to
those passages which seem to come from his preaching—in their general drift, if not necessarily in their precise wording. That degree of
reliability suffices for our purposes. A pattern of images can come
through, even where verbal expressions may fluctuate and change
somewhat.

(3) Beyond question, Jesus used some expressive language
which others had provided. He inherited a rich and diverse store-
house of imagery which he could adopt and creatively employ. The
imagery drawn from the past appeared both to liberate—not block—
his originality and to serve his strongly individual style of preaching.
Nevertheless, I am not trying here to assess his degree of originality.

The question is *not*: How uniquely inventive did Jesus show himself in his language? Rather my question is: What does the imagery used by Jesus suggest about the way his sensibility functioned?

(4) Let me add a final remark for readers nervous about orthodoxy. I am not discussing, let alone calling into question, Jesus' divine identity. All the same, no appeal to his status as the Word of God become flesh will tell us anything significant about the actual ways in which his human imagination operated. We may get some clues about that from the material in the gospels.

Features of Jesus' Imagination

After noting these major presuppositions, let us come back to the case being argued. The preaching of Jesus lets us glimpse the flow and flavour of the imagination which took shape during the hidden life at Nazareth. We can pick out four features of his imagery.

(1) First, Jesus shows himself aware of and responsive to *a broad range of human activity, suffering and happiness.* He notes how farmers fatten calves for a feast, and knows that bumper harvests may call for extra barns. If he offers no suggestions about thistle control and the removal of rocks, he realizes that poor terrain can reduce the results of seeding. He recalls how people arrange parties, organise ceremonies and behave at feasts. He has watched people putting patches on torn cloaks and using fresh wineskins for new wine. Jesus knows, too, popular ways for forecasting the weather: 'When you see a cloud rising in the west, you say at once, "A shower is coming"; and so it happens. And when you see the south wind blowing, you say, "There will be scorching heat"; and so it happens' (Lk 12, 5ff).

Jesus does not flinch from facing human suffering. One of his most memorable stories features a traveler who is robbed, beaten up and left half-dead on a country roadside. He points to the greed of rich men which allows them to over-indulge, although sick beggars may lie starving in the streets outside. Human happiness does not pass Jesus by: the joy of a father whose renegade son returns, the celebrations at weddings, a housewife delighted to have recovered some missing money.

All in all, Jesus speaks of a wide range of human activity; the role of stewards in large households, the administration of the law, the price of sparrows in the market, the right recipe for mixing yeast with flour, poor building practices, financial investments, and much else besides. *The language of Jesus suggests an imagination that has scanned a great deal of normal human living.* If we gathered together all his images, we would have a reasonably detailed sketch of daily life in ancient Galilee.

(2) The preaching of Jesus tells the story of his imagination in a second way. His sensibility seems to have its *preferences.* He uses, for instance, a large number of farming images, which may seem surprising. He draws many illustrations, not from carpentry, but from agriculture and the care of cattle. He knows that donkeys and oxen need to be taken every day to water. These animals at times fall down wells and must be rescued even on the sabbath. Jesus notes that cultivating the soil and adding fertiliser might revitalise a barren fig tree. Farmers may buy up to five yoke of oxen. Gentile farmers keep pigs and feed them on pods. Piling up manure heaps, growing mulberry trees, gathering crops from the fields, separating wheat from darnel, minding sheep, ploughing the land—references to these and other farming activities dot the preaching of Jesus.

(3) For the most part, Jesus reveals an imagination that has grown to be sensitively aware of what is going on in his world. Nevertheless, there are *some gaps in the picture.* And this is my third point about his imagery. He delights in children, but he has next to nothing to say about the mother-child relationship. Occasionally he glances at the father-child relationship: 'What father among you, if his son asks him for a fish, will instead of a fish give him a serpent; or if he asks for an egg will give him a scorpion?' (Lk 11, 11f). But Jesus somehow finds his way round the mother-child relationship almost without pausing to notice it. When his eye runs forward to the troubles to come, he sympathises over the sufferings that will afflict pregnant women and nursing mothers: 'Alas for women with child in those days, and for those who have children at the breast' (Mk 13, 17). Except for one or two such tangential remarks, Jesus bypasses the mother-child relationship. Did he have such an utterly untroubled relationship to his own mother that this intimate area of life produced nothing for his language? Does it take the 'grit' of some

tension in such areas to produce imaginative pearls? Whatever the reason, his preaching does not derive imagery from the mother-child relationship.

Almost as remarkable is his silence about the husband-wife relationship. He defends married life by rejecting divorce, and insisting that even in their minds men should not go lusting after other men's wives. He speaks of marriage feasts, wedding guests and the maidens who waited for the bridegroom to fetch his bride from her parents' home to his own. But there the imagery stops. Nothing survives from the preaching of Jesus about the loving and caring life together of married people. To illustrate the nature of prayer Jesus tells a story about troubling one's neighbour at midnight to borrow some food:

> Which of you who has a friend will go to him at midnight and say to him: 'Friend, lend me three loaves; for a friend of mine has arrived on a journey, and I have nothing to set before him'; and he will answer from within: 'Do not bother me; the door is now shut, and my children are with me in bed; I cannot get up and give you anything'? I tell you, though he will not get up and give him anything because he is his friend, yet because of his importunity he will rise and give him whatever he needs (Lk 11, 5–8).

We might have expected the story to run: 'Do not bother me. The door is now shut, and my wife is with me in bed.' But Jesus has the man say: 'My children are with me in bed.'

Jesus differs from the scriptures he knows by not drawing images from the mother-child and husband-wife relationships. Isaiah, the psalms and other Old Testament books made childbirth a common simile: 'Like a woman with child, who writhes and cries out in her pangs, when she is near her time, so were we because of thee, O Lord' (Is 26, 17). Such imagery moves with natural ease to depict nursing mothers and growing babies:

> Rejoice with Jerusalem, and be glad for her,
> all you who love her. . . .
> You shall suck, you shall be carried upon her hip,
> and dandled upon her knees.

As one whom his mother comforts,
so I will comfort you (Is 66, 10–12)

The husband-wife relationship likewise turns up frequently among
Old Testament images—particularly to focus the disobedience of
God's people. Their idolatry and other sins grieved Yahweh as a
wife's infidelities grieve her husband. The sacred writers also saw the
positive possibilities in this comparison. Hosea celebrates God as the
tender lover who longs to woo his people. But none of this appears in
the gospel record.

Besides the mother-child and husband-wife-relationship, there
are other facets of human life that fail to get reflected in the language
and imagery of Jesus. He refers to the ravens and the lilies, goes to
the wilderness to pray and climbs mountains with his disciples. Nevertheless, his preaching reveals no delight in nature and natural
beauty. Nor does he indulge any pathos at the transience of things.
He is so busy urging his audience to live like genuine children of God
that he has no time to indulge wistful sadness at the world—still less
disillusionment with it. He could never make Vergil's sentiment his
own: 'There are tears for human affairs and mortal things touch the
mind (*sunt lacrimae rerum et mentem mortalia tangunt*).' Admittedly Jesus weeps over Jerusalem and shakes his head sadly: 'O Jerusalem, Jerusalem, killing the prophets and stoning those who are sent
to you! How often would I have gathered your children together as a
hen gathers her brood under her wings, and you would not' (Lk 13,
34). But, by and large, Jesus says little about his own failures and
perplexities.

Finally, images drawn from history, current world affairs and
geography hardly surface in the preaching of Jesus. There is a hereness and nowness about his language, a preoccupation with the scene
right in front of him. He recalls, of course, a few episodes from biblical history or myth like the story of the flood and the destruction of
Sodom. But Jesus betrays little interest in the past. He never mentions that founding event of Jewish history, the exodus from Egypt.
The Maccabean revolt, the Hasmonean period, the capture of Jerusalem by Pompey, the switch of Jewish allegiance to Julius Caesar, the
reign of Herod the Great (37-4 B.C.) and all the other crowded
events of recent history never even got a passing nod in Jesus'

preaching. That larger world of politics fails to come in sight. Apart from a brief remark about paying taxes to Caesar and a comment on some victims of Pilate's brutality, Jesus hardly even suggests that he is living under Roman rule. Once he draws a lesson from a military buildup—the king with ten thousand troops deciding not to risk war against a king with twenty thousand troops. But Jesus names no specific king nor any particular cold-war situation in the Mediterranean world of the first century. Another time he speaks vaguely of 'a nobleman' who 'went into a far country to receive kingly power and then return' (Lk 19, 12). But he mentions no historical figure as the peg onto which he hangs the parable of the pounds that follows. Jesus' mind reaches out to the immediate situation here and now. He neither scans history, not even the most recent history, nor lets his eye run around the Roman Empire for images and examples that he could press into service.

At times the message of Ezekiel and other classic prophets takes us around the world of their day: Persia, Egypt, Cyprus, Tarshish, Greece, southern Russia and a range of other places. But the known geography of his day provides little or no imagery for Jesus. His preaching does not even suggest that he lived near the Mediterranean.

To sum up: There is a hereness and a nowness about the language of Jesus, a preoccupation with the scene right in front of him. He does not share in that romantic imagination which revels in ancient times and far-away places.

So much for my third observation that the language of Jesus did not represent the whole of the world in which he lived. One could, of course, argue that his preaching did actually introduce historical references, included imagery drawn from the mother-child relationship and so forth, but the early Church and/or the evangelists censored out nearly all this language. One can only respond, however, that there are no plausible reasons for believing that such censorship took place. In general, we do best to work with what we have rather than speculate about missing material.

(4) Fourth, we throw away any right to comment on the way Jesus perceives reality, if we ignore *the earthy particularity* of his language. Characteristically, he answers general questions like 'Who is my neighbour?' by telling a story (Lk 10, 29–37). Of course, other

rabbis have done that—both before and after Jesus. But the fact that they can also display this habit does not make it any less his own. He thinks from below, not by way of deduction from above. He offers cases from which his audience can draw general principles if they want to. Even his generalising remarks stay close to earth: 'No one after drinking old wine desires new' (Lk 5, 39). There is a common touch in the proverbial sayings he cites: 'Doubtless you will quote to me this proverb: "Physician, heal yourself" ' (Lk 4, 23). He invites his hearers to perceive the particular things around them. His imagery is attuned to the earthy wisdom of ordinary people. All of this makes him the supreme preacher with the common touch. He speaks with us and to us, not merely at us.

To conclude: The imagery and language that Jesus uses suggests at least four conclusions about his sensibility. (1) A very wide range of things in his immediate environment catch his eye. If he is intensely aware of God, he also seems intensely aware of what he experiences on the human scene. (2) He has his preferences among the things he observes. (3) There are some surprising gaps in what he appears to notice. (4) His mind works from below—from the concrete case. In his own unique way he betrays the earthy wisdom of ordinary people.

The apocryphal gospels of early Christianity reflected popular curiosity about the hidden years of Jesus' life and indulged the imagination of their readers. It is more to the point, however, to reflect on Jesus' own imagination. The imagery that he employed gives a clue to the way his perception of the world worked. To move through his language to some insights into his sensibility can only be a real gain.

Notes

1. Naturally that encyclical also develops the theme of contemporary human experience.

2. Kasper, *Jesus der Christus* (Mainz, 1974), p. 44 (= *Jesus the Christ* [New York, 1976], p. 37; hereafter ET).

3. *The Man for Others* (London, 1964), p. ix.

4. In *The Christ* (London, 1972) Schoonenberg develops at length the difficulties that he (and others) find in the Chalcedonian pattern—at least as classical theology has understood it. See also 'Is Jesus "Man Plus God"?' *Theology Digest* 23 (1975), pp. 59–70.

5. *Christ sein* (Munich, 1974), p. 336 (= *On Being a Christian* [New York, 1976], p. 347; hereafter ET).

6. *Philosophical Fragments* (Princeton, 1962), p. 130.

7. *The Christ*, p. 63.

8. *Christ sein*, pp. 15ff. and 109ff. (= ET, pp. 25ff., 119ff.).

9. Paris, 1968 and 1972.

9a. Since Moltmann in *The Crucified God* and other works proposes a *Trinitarian* approach to the history of suffering, we could also describe his Christology as one 'from above'.

10. K. Rahner, 'On the Theology of the Incarnation', *Theological Investigations* 4 (London, 1974), p. 110.

11. *Christ sein*, p. 437 (= ET, p. 447).

12. *Jesus* (New York & London, 1979), p. 670.

13. *Theological Investigations* 4, pp. 130, 185; *Theological Dictionary* (New York, 1965), p. 402.

14. *The Human Face of God* (London, 1973), p. 148.

14a. In fairness to Robinson it should be noted that he has things to say about Jesus' suffering and, specifically, about the scene in Gethsemane. See his index of subjects under 'Gethsemane' (adding pp. 78f.) and 'suffering of Jesus' (adding pp. 40, 84, 232f.). However, on p. 233 we find Robinson confusing 'the place' of atonement with a (helpful) experiential 'starting-point' for explaining it. This allows him to dismiss the 'platform of the cross' as being 'for most people entirely remote'.

15. *Christ sein*, pp. 120–22; cf. p. 136 (= ET, pp. 128–30; cf. p. 144).
16. *Ibid.*, pp. 137–66 (= ET, pp. 145–74).
17. *Ibid.*, p. 152 (= ET, p. 160).
18. Luke describes Paul's encounter with the risen Lord on the Damascus road in 'heavenly', glorious terms. That meeting is quite unlike the meeting with the two disciples on the Emmaus road (Lk 24, 13–35).
19. *Christ sein*, pp. 342f. (= ET, pp. 353f.).
20. *Ibid.*, pp. 446f. (= ET, pp. 456f.).
21. 'The Problem of the Virginal Conception of Jesus', *The Virginal Conception and Bodily Resurrection of Jesus* (New York, 1973), pp. 21–68.
22. *Ibid.*, pp. 66f.
23. In *The Resurrection of Jesus Christ* (Valley Forge, 1973) I argue that 'with respect to resurrection faith, sheer reason and good sense alone fail to prove decisive' (p. 137; cf. pp. 63–74). On the evidence for the virginal conception see further R. Brown, *The Birth of the Messiah* (New York, 1977), pp. 517–33, especially pp. 527f.; see also my review in *Gregorianum* 59 (1978), pp. 756f.
24. *This Man Jesus* (New York, 1973), p. 134; italics mine.
25. *Christ sein*, pp. 150f. (= ET, pp. 158–60).
26. *This Man Jesus*, pp. 13ff.
27. *Christ sein*, pp. 325ff. (= ET, pp. 335ff.).
28. See further the Appendix: The Imagination of Jesus.
29. *Jesus der Christus*, p. 25 (= ET, p. 24).
30. *Christ sein*, p. 438 (= ET, p. 448).
31. *Jesus—God and Man* (Philadelphia & London, 1968), p. 350.
32. *Jesus* (London, 1974), p. 135; italics mine.
33. *Jesus ureigener Tod* (Freiburg, 1975), pp. 16–65; the author documents abundantly the German literature on the theme.
34. *This Man Jesus*, p. 80; italics mine.
35. This terminology comes from Kasper, *Jesus der Christus*, p. 141 (= ET, p. 120). It is also used by Schürmann and others.
36. *Jesus the Jew* (London, 1973), p. 224.
37. *Jesus*, pp. 310f.
38. R.E. Brown, *Crises Facing the Church* (London, 1975), pp. 34–36.
39. *Jesus der Christus*, p. 141 (= ET, p. 120).
40. *Christ sein*, pp. 175–83 (= ET, pp. 183–91).

41. *Jesus der Christus*, pp. 47f. (= ET, pp. 42f.).
42. *Ibid.*, p. 242 (= ET, pp. 205f.).
43. *Christ sein*, p. 381 (= ET, p. 391).
44. *Jesus der Christus*, pp. 256f. (= ET, pp. 216f.).
45. *Ibid.*, p. 256 (= ET, p. 216).
46. *Ibid.*, pp. 260ff. (= ET, pp. 219ff.).
47. *Christ sein*, pp. 411f. & 653 (= ET, pp. 421ff. & 666).
48. Postscript to E. Frank Tupper, *The Theology of Wolfhart Pannenberg* (London, 1974), p. 303.
49. *Jesus der Christus*, p. 15 (= ET, p. 16).
50. *Ibid.*, p. 48 (= ET, p. 43).
51. *Ibid.*, pp. 14f. (= ET, pp. 16f.).
52. *Christ sein*, p. 31 (= ET, p. 40).
53. *Ibid.*, p. 260 (= ET, pp. 270f.).
54. *Ibid.*, p. 116. (= ET, p. 124).
55. *Ibid.*, p. 203 (= ET, p. 212).
56. *Ibid.*, p. 142; see pp. 269, 273, 324, 334, 427, etc. (= ET, p. 150; see pp. 278, 283, 334, 345, 436f. etc.).
57. *Ibid.*, pp. 371–400, 418–26 (= ET, pp. 381–410, 428–36).
57a. H.W. Bartsch (ed.), *Kerygma and Myth* (New York, 1961), p. 39. But see also Bultmann's argument that the resurrection 'is far more than the resuscitation of a corpse' (*ibid.*, p. 40).
57b. 1 Tim 6, 13 does refer to Jesus' 'testimony before Pontius Pilate'. But like the majority of exegetes I do not believe that this letter comes directly from Paul himself.
58. *Jesus*, p. 74.
59. *Ibid.*, p. 8.
60. *This Man Jesus*, p. 28.
61. *Christ sein*, p. 152 (= ET, p. 166).
62. *Ibid.*, p. 153 (= ET, p. 161).
63. *Ibid.*, pp. 405f. (= ET, pp. 415f.).
64. *Ibid.*, p. 407 (= ET, pp. 416f.).
65. *Jesus*, p. 37.